"As one who has been involved in the project on Faith Development in the Adult Life Cycle since its beginnings in 1979, I am impressed with the way Ken Stokes has presented the results of the research, notably the differences between men and women and the crises and life changes of adulthood. Especially helpful is his discussion of the styles and stages of faith and the importance of doubt and questioning in the faith journey. In addition to good summaries of the works of James Fowler and John Westerhoff, he has presented Robert Havighurst's 'developmental tasks' and their implications for faith. I also appreciate the reflection questions and the optional group experiences for each chapter, which make the book eminently useful for study in any church or synagogue."

Rev. Boardman W. Kathan
Past General Secretary,
Religious Education Association
of the United States and Canada

"This is a book that both professionals and volunteers will find helpful. Dr. Stokes analyzes research findings in a practical way, making helpful and challenging pastoral recommendations for parishes, congregations, and synagogues. The emphasis on continuing development certainly makes 'faith' an active verb."

Loretta Girzaitis
Catholic Education Center
Saint Paul, Minnesota

"Kenneth Stokes's ability to take this research and apply it to the dynamics of adult faith development makes this book a significant contribution to the literature available to clergy and interested lay leaders. I appreciate the reflection questions and the various activities that Stokes has developed. Their inclusion in this book makes it all the more useful for use in congregational programming and study groups."

Rabbi Jerome Epstein
CEO The United Synagogue of America

D0205160

"We discover in surveys that many Americans give considerable thought to developing their faith, yet sometimes feel adrift in their efforts to make sense of what they are experiencing in their faith lives. Ken Stokes has written *Faith Is a Verb*, which will help such people, and the religious educators and counselors who seek to guide them. Drawing upon in-depth and national projectible surveys, earlier academic research, and his own long experience as a pastor, Ken Stokes sheds light on such vital questions as: What is the role of questioning in the development of faith? What changes in faith can we expect on the basis of age alone? What is the impact of life crisis on faith development?

"Stokes's book is carefully and clearly written, and has immediate practical application for anyone who seriously seeks to understand, and to build, his or her faith. Those who participate in small groups, for example, will find this book to be not only helpful and enlightening, but inspiring as well."

George Gallup, Jr.
The Gallup Organization, Inc.

"A wonderfully practical book about the nature of growing up in faith. Dr. Stokes has woven together solid research with a sound pastoral sense to create a resource that will benefit not only pastors, religious educators, and other ministers, but also anyone who desires more insight into the dimensions of mature belief."

Neil A. Parent
U.S.C.C. Catechesis/Faith Formation Division

Dynamics of Adult Faith Development

faith IS A verb

KENNETH STOKES

TWENTY-THIRD PUBLICATIONS

Mystic, Connecticut

Fourth printing 1992

Twenty-Third Publications
185 Willow Street
P.O. Box 180
Mystic, CT 06355
(203) 536-2611
800-321-0411

ISBN: 0-89622-397-3
Library of Congress Catalog Card No. 89-50156

PREFACE

This book is written for men and women—Catholic, Protestant, Jewish, or of another tradition—who may or may not be members of a parish, congregation, or synagogue but who are truly seeking to grow in their faith. It will have appeal, I believe, for those questioning readers who want to search out new meanings beyond the usual patterns of religious participation and find new understandings of their faith. Clergy, educators, counselors, and other leaders in the faith community who seek to help people in their faith development will also find it helpful.

The book is designed so that it can be read by an individual or by a group of people—class, study group, prayer circle—who will discuss it together. At the end of each chapter, there are several provocative *questions for reflection*. I hope readers will take the time to think about these questions individually and discuss them with others. In so doing, they will involve themselves in a dialogue with the author's ideas. Whether you agree or disagree with a concept or suggestion, you will grow in faith through this dialogue. That is the way true faith development takes place.

At the end of the book is a section of *optional exercises*, each related to one of the chapters, which will explore even more fully some of the extensions of the material in the text. These can be particularly helpful for classes or groups that may want to delve more deeply into each topic.

The Faith Development in the Adult Life Cycle Project

Throughout the text, reference is made to "the FD/ALC study." This project was conducted under the sponsorship of the Religious Education Association of the United States and Canada and 22 other national and regional denominations and religious organizations in the United States and Canada between 1981 and 1987. The "FD/ALC" acronym will save us all from repetitious references to the lengthy project title.

The FD/ALC study sought to identify and better understand relationships between the changing dynamics of adulthood and a person's developing individual faith. It was carried out through two very different research models, which we have called Module 1 and Module 2.

Module 1 was conducted by the Gallup Organization under the direction of its president, George Gallup, Jr., whose commitment to religious research is well known. It involved a 30-question telephone survey put to over 1000 people selected randomly throughout the United States. Module 1 findings have high statistical validity because of the Gallup Organization's experience and expertise in the field of data collection. The Module 1 report is a fascinating array of tables and statistics, and it tells us much about the attitudes of a cross section of people representing all ages, ethnic backgrounds, geographical lo-cations, and religious traditions.

Module 2 approached the research very differently. Whereas the Module 1 questions had to have simple "Yes" or "No," or multiple choice answers for statistical analysis, Module 2 asked open-ended questions. It gave the respondents the opportunity to flesh out their faith stories in their own words. Each of the 41 interviews lasted sev-eral hours and was transcribed so that both the psychosocial develop-ment and the faith development of the person interviewed could be analyzed. The Module 2 report is filled with a richness of personal il-lustration that complements Module 1's more statistical findings.

Before the project's final report was written, both Module 1 and Module 2 reports were reviewed and evaluated by over 900 religious practitioners and scholars at 14 regional conferences throughout the United States and Canada in 1985 and 1986. Their critiques and in-sights became significant factors in writing and publishing *Faith Devel-opment in the Adult Life Cycle: The Report of a Research Project* in 1987.

The scope of this little volume, and certainly of this Preface, prevents me from pursuing in more detail the many fascinating dimensions of the study. Those interested in reading the full *Report* can order it from Adult Faith Resources, whose address is at the end of this Preface.

Terminology and References
Since this book is written for people of all religious traditions, I've had some concerns about proper terminology that will have meaning for all. For example, the local faith community for Catholics is the parish, normally led by a priest; Protestants have congregations or churches with a minister or pastor as the leader; and Jews worship in a syna-gogue or temple under the leadership of a rabbi. My first thought was to include all three whenever a reference was made; then I decided to pick one generic term for all three traditions. Finally, I settled on a sort of literary mixture. On some pages, you will read about a pastor or a church. When you do, please translate it to the term most appropriate for you. In other situations, I consciously have used all three—"priest,

pastor, or rabbi"/"parish, congregation, or synagogue"—to remind us again that the suggestions in this book apply to all faith traditions.

When an entire book is mentioned, there is no footnote, since the complete listing for that book will be found in the bibliography at the end of this volume. When a specific reference is made, it is footnoted with the author's name and page number. Again, the full reference will be found in the bibliography.

Appreciation

This section is very difficult to write because I owe so much to so many for their contribution to *Faith Is a Verb*. I think particularly of the FD/ALC Project's Steering Committee, who provided oversight of the research itself. I remember with deep appreciation George Gallup, Jr., and his colleagues who contributed so much to our Module 1 research; and Connie Leean and Gwen Hawley who did the major research in Module 2. I reflect upon the countless insights and contributions of the leaders at our 1981 Symposium and the 1985-86 Regional Conferences, and the more than 1000 people who participated in them, each one bringing his or her special perspective to those exciting meetings. They all helped me pull together what was central and germane in the mass of research for the practical focus of this book. A little bit of all these people and countless others who, in letters and telephone calls, added new dimensions will, I hope, be found in these pages. I am deeply indebted to all of them!

At a very personal level, I express my deepest appreciation to Connie Davis, my secretary, who typed several drafts of the manuscript in and around her many other duties for Adult Faith Resources and, of course, my wife, Anne, who continued to live with me and support me emotionally even when deadlines and revisions played havoc with our family life.

And thank you, the reader, for considering the ideas in this book. It is my hope that they may open for you a new door or two in your faith development. If that be so, it will have served its purpose.

Kenneth Stokes
Adult Faith Resources
9709 Rich Road
Minneapolis, MN 55437

CONTENTS

Faith Is a Verb
Dynamics of Adult Faith Development

CHAPTER ONE

FAITH IS A VERB

The Concept of Faithing

THE SUNDAY BULLETIN ANNOUNCED PREPARATION sessions for those considering church membership. Chuck, a man in his forties, shared some of his feelings with a friend at the coffee hour following the service. "I'm not sure I'm ready to be a member of the church," he said hesitatingly. Then, looking his friend squarely in the eye, he continued, "The older I get, the more confused everything is. Hell, I'm asking questions now I never even *thought of* in confirmation class!"

Susan shared some of her feelings with friends in her prayer group, her eyes looking everywhere but at their faces. "I'm not sure what I believe anymore. I grew up in the church and thought I had a pretty strong faith, but now I feel like crossing my fingers when we say about half the parts of the creed." There was silence, then someone asked, "Don't you believe in the creed?" Again silence; then her words came slowly but obviously with profound honesty, "Well, I believe it for church; but I'm not sure I *really* believe it." Tears filled her eyes. "What's wrong with me? Am I losing my faith?"

Nothing is wrong with Susan, and it's okay for Chuck to be asking new faith questions in midlife (or even before...or after). What is unfortunate is that many of us have been taught that a creed, doctrine, or set of beliefs is inflexibly absolute, and to deviate from it is somehow wrong. Traditionally, churches have put a high premium upon conformity among their people and their major effort has been to maintain and enforce this conformity. Many of today's churches, however, have lessened the pressure. Catholicism has experienced Vatican II's "opening of windows" to new understandings; many Protestant groups emphasize the individual's taking ultimate responsibility for his or her own beliefs; contemporary Jewish leaders struggle to relate their tradition-based faith to the rapidly changing culture in which they must function.

The irony, well illustrated by Chuck and Susan's statements, is that many of us still *assume* that our church is demanding a stringent conformity. That may not necessarily be the case. For that matter, many wise and sensitive pastors, priests, and rabbis truly rejoice with those who take seriously the meaning of, and are actively seeking to grow in, their faith.

Over the 20 to 30 years of transition from childhood to full maturity, just about everything about us changes drastically. Our bodies begin to slow down, and flecks of gray hair and extra pounds appear without warning. We read books, attend continuing education classes, meet different kinds of people, and are continually stimulated by new concepts and understandings in our rapidly changing culture. Lindell Sawyers puts it this way in the film, *The Growth Dimension*:

> We are adults,
> in a world of change,
> without sure guidelines for the future.
>
> We are adults,
> who can learn,
> who can grow,
> who can choose a future,
> And begin to live it—now!

As individuals we change as we move through life.

At the same time, our world is changing. It has been said that today those over fifty have experienced more change in their lifetimes than in all the previous centuries of human history. Reflect, if you will, on the images of the decades: the *roaring* twenties; the *depression* of the thirties; the *world at war* in the forties; the *baby boom* of the fifties; Vietnam and the *rebellions* of the sixties; and where do we begin to categorize the seventies and the eighties? Morris Massey, in his book *The People Puzzle*, suggests that change over the lifespan involves interaction between a person's individual development *and* what is happening in society during the time this development is taking place. Therefore, a person growing up in the depression developed differently from a similar person growing up in the war years or during the sixties. We are, indeed, in many ways a product of our culture.

Okay, I've spent two paragraphs stating that we live in a world of rapid change. So what else is new? Hundreds of other writers have done so in more detail and certainly more adequately. I write these words to emphasize the paradox that, meanwhile, back in church, we somehow feel guilty when we find some interpretations and understandings of our personal faith changing. In the *Faith Development in the Adult Life Cycle* study, described in the Preface, we asked:

> Which of these statements best describes your own opinion:
>
> A person's faith *should not* change throughout life because it is the foundation for living.
> or
> A person's faith *should* change throughout life just as one's mind and body change.

The research team had expected close to a 50-50 split in the responses. Interestingly, a significant majority (65%) of those interviewed believed that a person's faith *should* change throughout life, while less than a third (32%) indicated that faith should *not* change. Most average, everyday people recognize that their faith does change, does grow, does develop as they move through life's journey. Yet, ironically, we still hear the phrases...

> "I'm probably wrong, but I believe that..."
> "I know it's in the creed, but I have real problems with..."
> "Don't tell the preacher, but I'm not sure I really believe the doctrine of..."

and, with Susan, "I believe it for church, but I'm not sure I *really* believe it." Why is it that we church people have to be so apologetic when we do some real thinking and praying, using our own God-given minds to create our own understandings of a faith that makes sense and can guide and direct our lives? And yet, we hear these expressions of guilt all the time in the church.

A closer look at the FD/ALC study's findings about people's responses regarding whether or not faith should change shows that a significantly larger number of church members (39%) than non-church members (24%) felt that faith should *not* change. For better or worse, the self-image of many church members suggests that, to be a good Catholic, Protestant, Jew, Evangelical, or Orthodox, growth and development in matters of faith is *not* good.

I react strongly to this image. It is the premise of this book that our faith should not be static or rigid or inflexible, but that the basic condition of being human is *to grow*. Just as our bodies, minds, and personalities change and develop, so the *spiritual dimension* of our lives must also mature.

Gail Sheehy's book, *Passages*, was on the bestseller lists for over two years in the late 1970s. Why? Because Sheehy helped us average, everyday people understand how patterns of change throughout the life journey were logical, legitimate, and normal. There are predictable "passages" that come to most persons as they move through their 20s, 30s, 40s and so on. So life, feelings, and values change—that's part of being human.

Unfortunately, *Passages* had very little to say about the way people's *faith* and religious understandings may change during the adult years. Sheehy focused primarily on physical and psychological, vocational and family change. Many church study groups using *Passages* felt that the dimension of "spiritual passages" was missing from the book. In many ways, that perception was a major catalyst behind the FD/ALC research and, ultimately, this book.

This concern emerged at a time, in the late 1970s, when an interest in the concept of *faith development* was also beginning to appear. The research and writings of theologian/educators James Fowler and John Westerhoff, in particular, emphasized a *dynamic*—growing, changing, developing—quality of faith rather than one that is absolute and unchanging. Both Fowler and Westerhoff suggest the phrase, "Faith is a verb," which provides the basis for the title of this volume and this chapter. Their contributions will be explored more fully in the next chapter.

"Faith is a verb" is a most intriguing concept and much more than a semantic gimmick. We all know that "faith" is a noun. According to the dictionary, a noun is a word that denotes or names a person, place, thing, quality, or act. Certainly "faith" is several of these. I have faith, you have faith; we sing "Faith of Our Fathers" (in recent years, "Faith of Our Parents") in services of worship; and most people would identify themselves as members of some particular faith. Most of us have never thought of, much less used, "faith" as anything but a noun.

But faith as a *verb* is intriguing. A verb is a word of action. The verb of a sentence indicates movement, activity, direction, purpose. There is a dynamic quality about a verb. A verb indicates *that something is happening.*

Now, I doubt if Fowler or Westerhoff or anyone else is seriously trying to suggest that we change English grammar. They are calling to our attention, however, that we must become fully aware of the dynamic quality, the *action* element, of "faith." Faith is more than a doctrine, belief, religious law, or creed. It is more than something we receive from God, or learn in a confirmation class, or profess in a Bar Mitzvah ceremony. Faith is always in process.

Faith is movement. To say, as we usually do, "I have faith," makes that faith totally passive...a thing I happen to *have*. It lacks the full quality of movement, creativity, and sense of development that is the goal of human life. "Faith is a verb" suggests new dimensions with tremendous potential for all of us.

Ask ten friends, or colleagues, or passersby on the street to define "faith" and you'll probably get ten different answers. (A friend suggested you'd probably get seventy, depending on the day of the week.) Does this mean that some definitions are right and others are wrong? No. It does mean, however, that each of us brings a unique, personal, individual understanding of the magnitude of what faith means to him or her. Is that heresy? I don't think so. It means that *my* faith is a unique blend of *my* background and *my* religious experience plus *my* development of body, mind, personality, social setting, and 1001 other dimensions of *my* being that make *me* unique and different from everybody else. Ultimately *my* faith must be owned by *me*!

Please don't misunderstand. The doctrines and traditions of the many different religions and denominations *are* important, for they help define those beliefs most commonly held by that group. However, they are but means to the end of helping the individual discover a personal faith that uniquely speaks to her or his individual spiritual needs. Creeds and doctrines are the *starting point* for meaningful faith development.

"Development." That's a key word. When writers like John Wester-hoff and James Fowler suggest that "faith is a verb," they are challenging us always to remember that faith has a *developmental* dimension, an action dimension, a quality of "verbness" too. In one sense, the concept of faith as developmental is really not new, but it is too often forgotten as we get caught up with the *proper* interpretation of scripture and the *correct* understandings of our belief systems. The concept of *faith development* has acquired high visibility among religious leaders since the late 1970s, primarily through Fowler's pioneering research and profound development of its basic concepts. Faith *development* is the recognition that faith is not static, but *dynamic*.

Let's explore this idea of "faith is a verb" a bit further. How does the idea sit with you, particularly if you're considering it for the first time? If you are like most of us (yours truly included), you'll probably feel awkward and uncomfortable saying "I faith," and "He or she faiths" (proper grammar) is even worse. Okay, what about this?

Try the word, and even more, the *concept* of "faithing." Still sound strange? Again, most of us have never used "faith" with an "ing" ending. However, think of all the action words we do use every day with no problem whatsoever:

"I am talk*ing*."
"He is snor*ing*."
"She is eat*ing* dinner."
"They are argu*ing* about petty things, and we are laugh*ing* at them."

Even in religious settings, we are "ing" ing all the time:

"The congregation is sing*ing* a hymn."
"The pastor is preach*ing* the sermon."
"The young man is pray*ing*."
"All of us are worship*ing*."

That's not so difficult. For that matter, those phrases and "ing" words come easily and logically. Well, then, why not this:

"As I get older, I realize that I am faith*ing* all the time."
"Most people in our parish help each other with their faith*ing*."

"Faithing" is not in the dictionary, but some day it may be. However, the word itself is less important than the *concept* that undergirds it...that faith is dynamic, not static: that it is an active and ever-becoming part of my life and yours...that it is always in process.

In the FD/ALC study, we found an interesting and very important paradox. Many persons interviewed, whose profiles indicated they were growing significantly in their faith, often stated that they felt they had "less faith" now than they had at age 16. Further analysis suggested this was primarily because they knew they had, consciously or unconsciously, rethought and modified many of the religious teachings of their childhood and youth. Although a person's faith actually is growing and maturing, he or she often perceives it as *diminishing* because such growth involves the rethinking, *and often rejection,* of traditional ideas. So, true faithing may be perceived by others, and often oneself, as negative because it necessitates change.

For some, all this may sound like theological "antics with semantics," so, in summary, let's state the point again clearly and positively. "Faith" is an enormously complex word that indicates a whole host of dimensions, running the gamut from traditional theology to contemporary psychology. Scholars have proposed a thousand definitions. Each has merit and each enriches our understanding of faith. But there is no "correct" definition of the term, other than in the mind of God. Ultimately, however, each of us must come to grips with the meaning of "faith" for her or his own life. All of us must find ways to synthesize our religious upbringing as it is tempered by the questioning spirit of later adolescence, a myriad of books, sermons, and discussions, and—probably of most importance—our life experiences, so that we can formulate what for each of us is an understanding of faith that can sustain and direct our lives. Every human being has this task...and that is "faithing."

"Faith" *is* a noun. It is a *thing.* It is that understanding of life's ultimate meaning that is central to every person's sense of identity and purpose for his or her life.

But "faith" is *also* a verb in the sense that it is never static and is always in process. When it ceases to be—when faith becomes the *unquestioned* acceptance of creed and dogma—that faith no longer has meaning for the living adult. My wife Anne wrote a term paper for a religion course in college entitled "What I Believe Today But Won't Guarantee I'll Believe Tomorrow." (She got an "A": sharp professor.) The title, and the paper itself, illustrate the concept of "faithing"—a process that is never ending.

In this little volume, I am exploring some of the dynamics of life's journey experienced by most adults. Adult educators strongly affirm the importance of *lifelong learning*. I propose that people of faith, similarly, strongly affirm the importance of *lifelong faithing*. As you read these pages, reflect upon how the ideas in them are similar to *or different from* your experience. You may not agree with everything you read, but even if you don't, you are engaging in a dialogue from which each of us will learn. In doing that, we are all in the process of *faithing*.

For Reflection

1. How do you react to the concept of "faithing"? If you have problems, is it difficulty with an unusual word, or something deeper? What are some of the positive aspects of the concept? How does it help us get a feel of the *dynamic* quality of our faith journey?

2. Have you ever felt like Chuck or Susan? Do you have a similar story? Did you ever feel guilty? Frustrated? Scared? How did you deal with these insecurities? What were some of the factors (such as reading a certain book, talking with someone, or personal reflection and prayer) that may have helped you work them through and grow in your faith?

3. As noted in the text, many of the persons interviewed in the FD/ALC study indicated a feeling of having "less faith" than when they were teenagers, but it was apparent that this was often because they had discarded faith concepts of their childhood as they, in truth, *grew* in their faith. Do you sometimes feel that way? Do you know others who do? Try to remember specific times, places, incidents, or issues. In what ways does this help you better understand your faith journey, your own process of *faithing*?

CHAPTER TWO

THE JOURNEY OF FAITH

Are There "Styles" or "Stages" of Faith?

LET'S LOOK IN ON A DISCUSSION taking place in...it could be a Catholic parish, a Protestant congregation, a Jewish synagogue, or an Orthodox church. What is important it that a group of people have come together at the appointed hour to study scripture. They are reading together the story of Creation in Genesis. More specifically, they are discussing the account of God's act of Creation in six days, followed by a day of rest (Genesis 1:1-2:4).

There are 15 members in the group, including the leader, but we focus on the conversation among four of them. Although they are good friends, their differences of interpretation of this passage are apparent. Let's listen.

Walt: Well, to me, this is a good example of the mythical stories ancient people created to explain natural phenomena that they couldn't understand. Since then, scientific knowledge has provided us with much more adequate answers. The Creation story is just that—a story. Why can't we just leave it there?

Verne: Yes, but do we have to assume that a "day" here in the Bible is only 24 hours? How do we know that the "days" of Creation might not have been a hundred years...or a thousand years? The Bible is very specific in speaking of days. That makes sense to me.

Mary: Why are you two arguing? Why should we even question the Bible? Its truth has been the belief of the church for centuries. Why, I'm willing to bet that if we took a survey of all the people in our church (parish, congregation, synagogue), more than half, probably three-quarters, of them would believe that God created the world in six days. That's good enough for me.

Ethel: You know, this discussion reminds me of Lawrence and Lee's wonderful play, *Inherit the Wind*. It's based on the Scopes Trial in the twenties, and portrays an intense courtroom debate between a literal interpretation of the Creation story and Darwin's theory of evolution. In the final scene, after everyone else has left, one of the lawyers picks up the two books that have symbolized these intensely different points of view—the *Bible* and Darwin. He holds each in one hand, balancing them up and down, then stops, puts *both* into his briefcase, and leaves the courtroom. Curtain! I guess that's where I stand. I need them both!

Verne: Well, I was taught in Sunday School to believe that God could do anything. For me...

Walt: (Interrupting) You know, Verne, I don't care what you were taught in Sunday School! *What do you believe now?* Why do we have to say we believe this story literally, when we all know it's not true? Science is science, religion is religion. Why mix them up?

Mary: Oh, Walter, you're always asking questions about religion. Why can't you just have faith like the rest of us?

Ethel: I think I understand your point of view, Walt. Your questions are good ones...ones *you* have to deal with, and they help all of us come to grips with where we are on some of these important matters of faith.

Think a bit about what each of these people is saying. If you had been a part of the group, what would you have said? With which of the four people do you feel you have most in common?

Perhaps you would like to make a few notes in the margin or on a piece of paper about your reactions. We're going to leave Verne, Mary, Ethel, and Walt now for a few pages, *but we'll come back to this conversation.*

In the first chapter, we looked at faith as developmental. Using the image of "faith is a verb," we emphasized the dynamic or action quality of faith, and suggested the concept of "faithing." In this chapter, we move to the next step in looking at faith development: is there a structure or a pattern to it?

Before anything else, I must begin by stating clearly that there is no universally accepted answer to that question. For some, faith is an absolute, a given that does not change; it is outside the individual, and one must either accept or reject it. For others, faith is so highly personal that there is no way it can be structured. For most of us who find meaning in the concept of faith development, however, there do seem to be some patterns. We will look at two theories, with some input from a third. Keep in mind, however, that these are not *the* stages or styles of faith development; they are attempts by some theologian/ educators to provide frameworks for understanding the concept of faith development. Other theories are being created every day, and we could write a book on all of them. However, for our purposes here, we'll focus on the two that are most widely known.

Westerhoff's Styles of Faith

In his book, *Will Our Children Have Faith?*, religious educator John Westerhoff uses the imagery of a tree's rings to suggest four different styles of faith. He reminds us that, as a tree grows, it adds rings to expand and mature, but the previously formed rings are still present in the central core of the tree's trunk. The four styles of faith are: *Experienced Faith, Affiliative Faith, Searching Faith,* and *Owned Faith.*

Experienced Faith

"Experience" is the basis of the earliest style of faith. Children have their first understanding of faith through experiences. Placing the baby Jesus in the manger creche or lighting the ceremonial candles for the Jewish sabbath meal are often the child's first experiences of his or her family's faith tradition. I can still remember, as a boy, spending several days before Christmas, "swimming" in my father's bathrobe, singing "We Three Kings" and marching the length of the living room to deposit, one after the other, a small wooden box with some coins in it, a bottle of perfume, and a lighted candle in front of the Christmas tree. (I had no idea what "frankincense" and "myrrh" were, but my mother suggested that the perfume and candle were pretty close.) I was *experiencing* a very basic element of my embryonic faith—honoring the Christ child.

A few years later, I went to church camp for the first time. As we sang around the fire and closed the day with a friendship circle ("right hand over left"), I experienced the power of ritual and sharing with others that is so important for personal faith. Questions of belief and doctrine were yet to come; for me—and I daresay for most of us—the beginnings of faith come in meaningful *experience*.

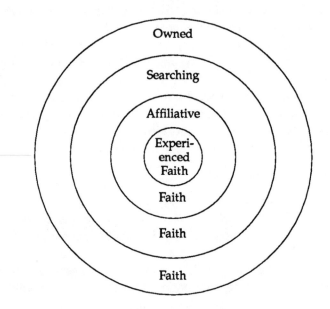

Affiliative Faith

Most people find the fullest expression of their faith in community. Whether it be the exhilaration of corporate worship on Easter or during the Jewish holidays, or those times of friendship and fellowship that follow a wedding or even a funeral, people find meaning in faith by being together. For Westerhoff, *affiliative* faith—the sense of belonging—is a vitally important next "ring" in the development of the individual's personal faith. It takes a variety of forms—confirmation in most Christian churches, bar and bat mitzvah in the Jewish tradition. The *affiliative* dimension is the logical extension of the experience of faith.

What pride there is when a young man or woman becomes an *adult* member of the faith community. I stood at the front of the congregation and was welcomed, and my name was put in the church bulletin. Shortly thereafter, we had a meeting of the congregation and I was able to vote. Even filling out the pledge card and receiving adult offering envelopes was an important step in my faith, because I knew *I belonged.*

Searching Faith

For most of us, usually in late adolescence and young adulthood, however, education and a broadening world view often lead us to doubt and question some of those values so fundamental to our earlier understandings of faith. Parents seem a bit "out of touch" with our needs. Our own sense of self as an adult is beginning to emerge and, with Paul, we tend to "put away childish things." Westerhoff states it simply:

> In order to move from an understanding of faith that belongs to the community to an understanding of faith that is our own, we need to count and question that faith.[1]

Thus emerges the next ring in the individual's tree of faith: a faith that is *searching* for new meaning. This is not always an easy transition. Often parents, clergy, and members of our religious tradition chastise us for "losing faith." In the intensity of our searching, we can become abrasive and dogmatic in our reaction to the faith traditions we have known. Sometimes, we will withdraw from active participation in the church or synagogue. For some it is temporary; for others, sadly, it may last for years, or forever.

However difficult it may be for self and others, though, for an individual truly to mature in personal faith, some experience of *searching* for a new fullness of meaning is necessary.

Owned Faith

The last, but also the largest ring in Westerhoff's model of the tree of faith comes when *searching faith* finds maturity in one's *owned faith.*

Here, faith moves beyond experience, affiliation, and searching to become a central and vital part of the person's total being. It is a part of reaching one's full potential. For some, it comes in an identifiable and often dramatic experience of conversion; for others, it grows quietly and often slowly until the individual becomes aware that, although some faith may be shared with others, personal faith is now her or his very own.

> A priest, a minister, and a rabbi were having a theological discussion. Predictably, they found they could not agree at all points in the dialogue ("trialogue" would be better), but they thoroughly enjoyed the stimulating exchange of ideas. Finally, they had to adjourn and go their separate ways. As they were leaving, one of them said to the others, "Well, friends, it's been great. Isn't it wonderful that we're all doing God's word—you in your ways...and I in his!"

They all laughed and left the room arm in arm, the other two wishing they had said it.

A funny story, yes. However, it symbolizes a far deeper and more important point: we can respect and rejoice in the faith expression of others; we can learn from faith traditions not our own; and we can feel that sense of interfaith community that binds us together. But, deep down inside, the *owned faith* of the individual is the fullest expression of God's power and love. In a sense, I *must* believe that *my* faith expresses God's way *for me*. Only then is my faith maturing and am I truly faithing.

Westerhoff presents and develops these four styles of faith in but 15 pages of his book, but they capture with vigor and vitality a simple but profound image of how faith, like the rings of a tree, may develop.

Fowler's Stages of Faith

Undoubtedly, the most profound contribution to the field of faith development in the 1970s and 1980s has been made by James Fowler. Although he has written or edited several books on the topic, his central theory is most fully developed in *Stages of Faith*. Based on extensive interviews with more than 500 persons, Fowler provides a theory of *stages* of faith development that is solidly grounded theologically but intriguingly simple in outline. We can in no way explore the richness and depth of his theories in these few pages. However, the importance of his contribution demands an exploration of its basic structures. What follows, then, is a simplified overview presented with commentary on some significant aspects of the theory. (Those wishing to explore the concept more fully are urged to read *Stages of Faith*.)

Faith, according to Fowler, is not something that one does or does not have. It is, rather, a process of *becoming*, hence the concept of "faith is a verb" discussed in our first chapter. This process is continually growing through stages that are "hierarchical" (increasingly complex and qualitative), "sequential" (they appear one after the other in life span), and "invariant" (they follow in the same order for all persons).

Fowler sees an individual's faith journey moving through six stages. Few persons progress through all six, and many only progress through two or three. Each person, however, finds that "stage" of faith that has the fullest meaning for him or her. The person may remain there throughout life, or may move through several stages during the life cycle. The task of the faith community is to find a proper balance between accepting and respecting people's present faith stages and yet encouraging them in the exploration of other stages. Fowler has ascribed descriptive terms to each stage, and we use this terminology. However, most discussions of the Fowler stage theory use the numbers 1-6 to indicate the stages, so we will use them also.

I have also added, in parentheses, descriptive titles that I believe are helpful for each stage. These descriptive titles come from Charles McCollough's book, *Heads of Heaven; Feet of Clay*. Although they are not Fowler's terms, each provides a succinct descriptive word for each stage.

Stage 1: Intuitive-Projective Faith (The Innocent)
This stage is found in pre-school children and is primarily a reflection of parental faith. What understanding the child may have of God is essentially that learned from parents; if there is no discussion of the subject in a family context, most children will have little concept of any meaning for the term. Similarly, if grace is said before meals, the child experiences something of a rudimentary meaning of prayer; if grace is not said, then that child's faith takes a different dimension.

Stage 1 is filled with fantasy, imagination, and powerful images, and these play an important part in the child's first understanding of faith. But, it is still essentially a faith understood through the family experience. We probably would not ask pre-schoolers to describe their faith, but this dialogue might be very appropriate:

    Adult: "What church do you go to, Stevie?"

> *Stevie:*   "We go to the (denomination) church."
>
> *Adult:*   "Tell me, why do you go to the (denomination) church?"
>
> *Stevie:*   "Because Mommy and Daddy go to that church."

As the twig is bent, the tree is inclined.

Stage 2: Mythic-Literal Faith (The Literalist)

This stage usually begins about age 6 and normally lasts until about 11 or 12. In it, the child's understanding of faith is still essentially a reflection of the concepts and beliefs of others, but the circle has widened from the family to include the influence of other adults—teachers, coaches, older friends—and often older children. It is during this period that the children become aware of the many, often confusing, interpretations of faith. Protestants become aware of Catholics, and vice versa; the traditions of Hanukkah and Christmas are compared and celebrated in public schools. The child's faith begins to broaden, but the understanding of faith is still primarily within the context of family and other trusted older persons.

Religious images are often understood literally. A youngster asks her father the eternal question:

> *Debra:*   "Daddy, where's God?"
>
> *Daddy:*   "Honey, we believe that God is everywhere."
>
> *Debra:*   "Is God in this house, then?"
>
> *Daddy:*   "Yes, dear, God is in this house."
>
> *Debra:*   "Daddy, is God in this room?"
>
> *Daddy:*   "Well, yes, honey, I think God is in this room."

Debra goes to the kitchen sink and takes a cup off the shelf, and points into it.

> *Debra:*   "Then God is in this cup?"

Now Daddy has painted himself into a rather interesting theological corner, but his answer is consistent, at least.

> *Daddy:*   "Yes, Debra. I think God is...in some ways...in that cup."

Debra holds the cup in the air, eyeing it critically. Then quickly a smile crosses her face, she places her hand firmly across the top of the cup, and exults:

> "Goody! I've got him!"

Stage 2 children usually take their faith interpretations quite literally. They love the stories from the Bible—Noah's Ark, Jonah and the Whale, David and Goliath, etc. Deeper symbolism is not yet there, but the religious imagery is often very real.

We also find Stage 2 in adult colleagues and friends. They are those whose faith is straightforward and often quite literalistic. They usually have a strong sense of the *authority* of the biblical narratives and religious tradition. For example, look back to the Bible study discussion at the beginning of this chapter. Verne is an example of a Stage 2 adult. He accepts the literal meaning of a "day" in creation, even if it must mean defining it differently from a 24-hour period. Further, the basis of his firmly held belief is that "...I was taught in Sunday School to believe that...."

Stage 2 adults often find the fullest expression of their faith in those churches that emphasize a more literal interpretation of scripture. When involved in discussions about matters of faith with friends holding different perspectives, they often are frustrated because they feel that person does not see the *true* faith, and they can exert a good bit of energy trying to convince and convert.

There is a simplicity and security about a Stage 2 faith. For some, it is a basis for a lifetime of deep conviction and commitment. For others, it is a starting point for new explorations of faith.

Stage 3: Synthetic-Conventional Faith (The Loyalist)
Stage 3 usually appears in adolescence, but is also highly visible in adulthood. Let's look at each separately.

In the growing years, Stage 3 is the junior-high stage. This is the "gang" age. Your 12-year-old daughter wants to go out with the "gang" on Friday. You ask here where they're going. "Oh, we don't have any definite plans," she says. "Whatever the gang wants to do, we'll do." They may end up playing frisbee in the park or drinking milkshakes at the ice cream shop. Where or what they are doing is not all that important. What is important is doing it *with the group*. There is a negative side also. The adolescent who does *not* identify with some group of peers usually feels lonely and rejected. The peer relationship is vitally important in this period of life.

And so with faith development. You are the leader of a confirmation class, or other religious education group of adolescents. You ask Billy to describe his understanding of what God is like. Billy stumbles and stammers, and what he says may not be theologically sophisticated, but he makes a genuine effort and comes up with a plausible response. You thank Billy, and turn to another member of the group, "How would you put it, Ginger?" Ginger smiles, looks away, then counters, "I guess I agree with Billy. Yes, I think he said it pretty well." You notice that several heads around the circle are bobbing up and down.

Agreement and conformity are paramount; what is important, even in matters of faith, is the approval of peers. The security of a community of like believers provides the context of faith that is vital. Our commitment to strong youth ministry is based on our understanding that adolescents' faith development takes place best in the context of a group. Summer camp or the winter ski outing provide opportunities for that mixture of fun, discussion, reflection, worship...*and faithing* that takes place most fully in relationship with one's peers.

Among adults, Stage 3 is the stage most commonly found among church members, according to Fowler's research. Why not? That's why we have parishes and synagogues and congregations in which people can find some common faith identity. Stage 3 adults express their faith in the context of that community of believers to which they relate. One's faith is described by saying something like "We Catholics (or Jews, or Lutherans, or whatever) believe...." It places a strong emphasis on those creeds and doctrines and traditions that are the expected norms for membership in that particular group. That's good. The Faith Stage 3 person needs this strong sense of community. Most find meaning in their faith as they share beliefs and understandings with others with whom they essentially agree. Their authority is no longer parents or teachers; it is that community of like-minded believers of which they feel a part.

Let's go back again to the discussion at the beginning of the chapter. Mary symbolizes the Stage 3s of the group. Her suggestion about interpreting the six days of Creation is to survey the congregation. What is important to Mary is consensus of belief within the faith community.

Later, she responds to Walt's questioning with intensity. "Why can't you just have *faith* like the rest of us?" For Mary, "faith" comes in agreement and harmony. Disagreements or disharmony are obstructions to faith. For many, like Mary, to question or to digress from the norm undercuts that powerful sense of community that is central in the faithing process.

Most people's faith is Stage 3 faith. For most people, their expression of faith is an extension of those beliefs most commonly held by their own church or synagogue, or significant peer group. In the Fowler schema, this is a part of an ongoing faith journey through the stages. For many people, however, it is the expression of faith that has adequate and full meaning throughout their spiritual lives.

Stage 4: Individuative-Reflective Faith (The Critic)
Somewhere in the later teen years, our son or daughter will come to the dinner table and say something like "Mom, I don't know if I believe in God any more!" or, "Dad, I don't think I'll be going to church with you for a while. I've got to work some things out *for myself.*"

We parents react in a variety of ways. Too often, we express shock; we feel we've failed as parents, and the like. Actually, we should rejoice, for our "child" is beginning to grow up. At that time in life's developmental pattern, our son or daughter is not only beginning to deal with matters of vocation, lifestyle, and values identity, but is also beginning to *take charge* of his or her own faithing. As a part of taking responsibility for one's own life, the young adult is also beginning to ask questions about life's ultimate meaning—questions of faith. This is not always easy. It involves doubting, struggling with new concepts, and even sometimes *rejecting* traditional assumptions. But, it is an important *and necessary* step for maturing faith.

Stage 4 may take bizarre forms, for a while, such as participation in cult movements or even expressions of atheism, but these are a part of a process of finding one's own faith. For most of us, however, it is not permanent, but a necessary transition in the process of maturing spiritually.

Stage 4 is not limited to the young adult years. For that matter, the FD/ALC study showed Stage 4 responses throughout the life span, with a significant number in the middle years. Unfortunately, we also found many cases of disillusionment with the established church among mature men and women who had gone to their rabbi, priest, or pastor with serious, hard questions of faith and belief, only to be told that "you mustn't question your faith" or some similar statement. The research points up the uncomfortable truth that countless men and women have simply opted out of the established religious community when they found that clergy and fellow church members were unwilling to take seriously the concerns, questions, and even doubts that they raised with a sincere desire to better understand. As one young woman put it, "It's tough being Stage 4 when you're surrounded by Stage 3 parents and preachers."

In the scenario at the beginning of the chapter, Walt is somewhat typical of people in Faith Stage 4. He sincerely questions the traditional interpretations, looking for alternatives that he can explain rationally in the context of his contemporary world view. He is abrasive in his challenge to Verne: "I don't care what you were taught in Sunday

School! What do you believe now?" because he cannot understand why Verne is not asking similar questions. (Such abrasiveness is not *necessarily* a component of Stage 4, but the tendency to question established positions does tend to set many Stage 4s somewhat at odds with others.) Obviously, Mary's response to Walt evidences a frustration with his questioning and, from her perspective, *lack* of faith. If Walt had been in a good mood and had just finished reading Fowler, he might have responded with a smile, "But, Mary, I'm going through my Stage 4 faith development transition!"

Faith Stage 4 is *not* a comfortable stage. One does not usually stay in it for lengthy periods. In the logical progression of faith development, Stage 4 leads to Stage 5. In other cases, the struggles of Stage 4 lead to a return to the relative security of Stage 3 or even Stage 2. For others, unresolved questioning during one's Stage 4 period can lead to a complete opting out of any conscious or direct dealing with faith issues.

The concept of Stage 4 in Fowler's schema, and the Searching Faith style of Westerhoff are of central importance in faith development, since they affirm that the fullness of maturity in one's faith *must include* some dissonance of doubt and the facing of hard questions that often move against the current of popular belief. It is unfortunate that so many people—clergy and laity alike—view the questioning stance from the negative perspective of "losing one's faith" rather than the positive affirmation of a person who is truly taking charge of her or his faithing and seeking answers that will provide the fullest possible dimension of a meaningful personal faith.

We will look further at some elements of Stage 4 in the next chapter.

Stage 5: Conjunctive Faith (The Seer)

Fowler's Faith Stage 5 seldom appears before age 30, since maturity is a major ingredient in its development. It draws together several strands of the individual's faith journey—family upbringing, previous religious affiliation (if any), and the influences of education, social context, and lifestyle upon them. Put simply, a Stage 5 person builds on his or her previous faith journey through Stages 1-4, integrating elements of each into an understanding of faith that is uniquely his or hers. This faith may well be similar to that which was held earlier in the faith journey, but the uniqueness of Stage 5 comes in the fact that now one's faith expression is no longer that of parents, church, or tradition, but is now clearly *one's own*. "Our faith" becomes "my faith." It is an "owned" faith, which is precisely the term used by Westerhoff for the parallel style of his construct.

One of the most significant aspects of Stage 5 persons is the ability to see perspectives other than their own. Stage 5 Catholics, for example, may not accept all tenets of Protestantism, but they are able to discuss faith issues with Protestant friends with sensitivity to and affirmation of the other person's positions. Hence, Ethel, who, in our dialogue symbolizes Stage 5, retells the incidents from *Inherit the Wind* to try to illustrate that there is merit on *both* sides of the issue. Even though she does not totally agree with Walt's position, Ethel expresses her understanding of and appreciation for his perspective, and thanks him for helping the group by his contribution. Whereas Verne and Mary seem to be irritated with Walt's intensity, Ethel is genuinely able to affirm him, since she has been there and recognizes the importance, for him, of his deep concerns.

Persons in Faith Stage 5 are able to identify with people of different races, socio-economic status, or ideological conviction. They find meaning and fulfillment in cross-cultural experiences. Working with farmers in Central America or coaching a ball team of underprivileged youngsters in the inner city symbolize the kinds of faith expressions embraced by many Stage 5 persons.

From a slightly different perspective, the Stage 5 individual's faith structures know few bounds. A Christian may participate in the scripture study group at the local synagogue, not in anticipation of becoming a Jew, but for the spiritual broadening of self that comes from experiencing faith in contexts other than one's own. Or, a Stage 5 Protestant whose faith has been primarily expressed through social activism and church involvement may opt for a period of time apart for spiritual renewal at a Catholic retreat center.

The axiom of education, "The more you learn, the more you know how much you do *not* know," has a parallel application here. The maturing Stage 5 person becomes increasingly aware of the seemingly unending possibilities that open up challenging and enriching new opportunities for spiritual growth through faithing, and the potential meaning of faith becomes limitless.

The central element of Faith Stage 5 comes, as has already been noted but needs to be reiterated, in Westerhoff's word and concept of "owned" faith. Those persons have discovered a dimension of faith expression that is truly their *own*. It may come in song, or in writing, or in spoken words. For some, it can emphasize theological concepts, while for others it may be found in ways of simple living. It does not *necessarily* deviate from traditional experiences of faith, and may well be quite orthodox. What is important is that the Stage 5 person has come to this point in her or his faithing ultimately by his or her own decision, and not the pressures of others. Some Stage 5s become more active in their churches, while others may well seek out different contexts for expressing their faith. Stage 5 faith is many-faceted; it has an infinite variety of expressions. It usually comes in the fullness of life, and for those who experience it, it can and often does become the most important dimension of their lives.

Stage 6: Universalizing Faith (The Saint)

It many ways, Stage 6 is the most difficult stage to understand, and yet, without it, a necessary dimension of the theory would be lacking. Fowler himself has referred to Stage 6 as "at best a kind of abstract poetry." However, his research repeatedly finds that there is a small group—perhaps one or two percent of the population—whose faith is more than beliefs or even a way of life, but is one of *total commitment* to the ongoing, guiding presence of God or whatever the person recognizes as Ultimate Authority.

The Faith Stage 6 person is motivated by the guiding sense of this Ultimate Authority in all aspects of life. We are reminded of Jesus in the Garden: "Father, if thou art willing, remove this cup from me; nevertheless *not my will but thine be done*" (Luke 22:42 RSV). Jesus did not want to go to the cross. He probably wanted to continue his ministry of teaching and healing. But his greater commitment was that *God's will be done*. The faith of a Stage 6 person is similar. That faith goes beyond belief or even a fully developed personal faith. It is a faith of total commitment to that person's Ultimate Authority.

Fowler lifts up familiar names as people he considers representatives of Faith Stage 6: Gandhi, Martin Luther King, Jr., Mother Teresa, Dag Hammarskjold, Dietrich Bonhoeffer, Abraham Heschel, and Thomas Merton, to name a few. And there are many others, most of whom do not win Nobel Peace Prizes and, for that matter, may hardly be known beyond their own communities. Their faith, however, is that of total commitment, even—if necessary—to death. There are very few Stage 6s, but they are there and cannot be overlooked. For Fowler, Stage 6 symbolizes the ultimate fulfillment of one's faith journey.

This overview of Fowler's stage theory of faith development does not do justice to the sensitive complexity of his design. For example, there are seven aspects of each stage, there is the dynamic of *transition between* stages, and the totality is provocatively rich and full in a multiplicity of dimensions similar to the way a simple tune is developed into the fullness and majesty of a great symphony. However, it is hoped that these pages provide an understanding of the *basic* elements of the theory with illustrations of its meaning for adult life. As has already been stated, those who wish to explore it more fully are urged to do so.

A Problem with Stages

Some people feel uncomfortable with the concept of stages. They feel that stage theory conforms an individual into a structural pattern that is purely theoretical. They feel it constructs an artificial hierarchy—a climb up the "spiritual ladder"—which suggests that some people are "more spiritual" than others. Stages, they argue, suggest an ideal that can never be fully realized.

They are uneasy about categorizing people. Even the discussion presented at the beginning and alluded to throughout this chapter with the suggestion that Verne, Mary, Walt, and Ethel may symbolize Faith Stages 2, 3, 4, and 5 will trouble some readers. Whereas it is my purpose to suggest them merely as *illustrations,* some will argue that it is presumptuous to try to define an individual's faith so simplistically. To these persons, I accept and recognize their argument, but suggest another perspective.

The educator in all of us recognizes individual differences and needs. Some people attend a study group on "Introduction to the Bible" because they are near the beginning of their faith journey, while others respond to cognitive discussions of theological issues, and still others find fullest meaning in personal reflection and prayer. Different people *are* at different places in the development of their faith (in their *faithing*), and to recognize this is not necessarily a judgment that, in any way, one has *more* faith than another. Mary (Stage 3) is not "more faithful" than Verne (Stage 2) nor is Ethel (Stage 5) faithing more fully than Walt (Stage 4). Each is at a point along faith's developmental journey, and experiences the dimension of faithing appropriate for that stage. As people of faith, it is for each of us to help those persons with whom we have contact to "bloom where they are planted," to paraphrase the popular poster, and to mature in faith at their own pace in an appropriate way.

Faith stages remind us that there are not so much "rights" and "wrongs" in matters of faith as there are individual differences of development and interpretation, *each of which may well be the most valid expression of faith for that individual.*

Fowler's theory touches a nerve of truth. It provides a framework for understanding a phenomenon that many of us have observed for years: that people *do* deal with matters of faith in a variety of ways. An understanding of this variety not only will help each of us in our own faith development, but also make us more sensitive to an understanding of the faith of others.

A Synthesis

The theories of Westerhoff and Fowler, presented in this chapter, plus the descriptive titles suggested by McCullough, *taken together,* suggest a framework which can be helpful in our understanding of how faith may develop. To summarize this chapter, we can put them together in this way:

WESTERHOFF	FOWLER	McCULLOUGH
Experienced Faith	Stage 1: Intuitive-Projective Faith	The Innocent
Experienced Faith	Stage 2: Mythical-Literal Faith	The Literalist
Affiliative Faith	Stage 3: Synthetic-Conventional Faith	The Loyalist
Searching Faith	Stage 4: Individuative-Reflective Faith	The Critic
Owned Faith	Stage 5: Conjunctive Faith	The Seer
Owned Faith	Stage 6: Universalizing Faith	The Saint

Are there really "styles" or "stages" of faith? If so, are these theories "on target," or are there other ways to describe the process of faithing? Regardless of our answer, they do help us get a handle on the concept of faith as a verb, of faith as becoming, of *faith as a journey.* If they help us better understand our own faith journey, and something of the journeys of those close to us, then they are a step in the right direction.

For Reflection

1. Do you see "styles" or "stages" in your own faith journey? Can you identify some events or experiences that provided transitions from one to another? If you have ever moved from one style or stage to

another, then back to the previous one, what was that like? Where do you see yourself *now* in your faith journey?

2. How can we see the values of growing and maturing in faith without falling into the trap of viewing the styles or stages of faith development as a "ladder of achievement"? In what ways can we encourage others in their faith development, yet not pressure them into a style or stage that may not be appropriate for them at this time?

3. Reread the dialogue at the beginning of the chapter and its use as illustration throughout the chapter. Do you know or have known "Vernes," "Marys," "Walts," or "Ethels" in your life? Reflect yourself or describe to someone else a group experience in which different styles/stages of faith were represented. How do these theories better help you understand the dynamics of this experience?

4. What other implications, problems, possibilities do you see arising from an understanding of style/stage theory of faith development in your home? In your church, parish, or synagogue? In your relationship with others?

CHAPTER THREE

"BUT, WHAT IF...?"

*The Role of Doubt
and Questioning in Faith*

REFLECT AGAIN, IF YOU WILL, ON THE FIRST PAGE of Chapter One. If you are a pastor, priest, rabbi, or religious counselor, reflect a bit on how you would respond to Chuck's "I'm asking questions..." or Susan's "Am I losing my faith?" If you belong to a parish, synagogue, local church, how do you think your pastor, priest, or rabbi would respond to them?

These questions are not posed to put religious leaders on the defensive. Frankly, I do believe that most pastors today would respond with empathy, loving concern, and a sincere desire to help the questioner. Spiritual leaders must play a dual role in situations like these. On one hand, they are counselors seeking to help people like Chuck and Susan deal with real personal problems. At the same time, however, they also must seek to interpret clearly the traditions and beliefs of the faith community they represent. The pastor's response may well run the gamut from the highly non-directive "How do you feel about it? What do *you* believe?" to the more authoritarian "But our faith expects us to believe, to accept many things without questioning them. You mustn't doubt your faith!"

So, this presents a very real problem for many contemporary people. What *is* the role of questioning and doubt in one's growing faith? For many, "doubt" is synonymous with *disbelief*; it is the rejection of faith. To question or struggle with one's faith is negative. It marks a person as one who has "fallen away" from the true practice of his or her faith—something to be avoided like the plague. Yet, in a larger sense, questioning and doubt may well be the *key* to one's faith development. In many ways, doubt and questioning are, for many of us, integral and necessary aspects of our faithing.

Let's be more specific. Doubt and questioning have been around since the beginning of time. The stories of the patriarchs are filled with questioning of God's directives. Moses questioned the leadership role placed on his shoulders. Job agonized to understand the tragedies that plagued him. Thomas, the questioning disciple, demanded proof of Jesus' resurrection, and the term "doubting Thomas" remains with us to this day. Paul resisted the Christian faith and persecuted its followers until his own conversion.

Religious history is filled with the faith struggles of many of its greatest leaders—Augustine, Joan of Arc, Martin Luther, Abraham Heschel, Albert Schweitzer, Dietrich Bonhoeffer, Hans Küng, and countless others—who dared to doubt...and question...and challenge established beliefs and traditions. Because they did, their faith and the faith of those who followed them was made stronger.

Many of us today wrestle with questions and issues that put us in conflict with our own religious tradition. These can run the gamut from biblical interpretation ("Did those miracles really happen as written?"), to historic doctrine ("Was Jesus truly God in human form?"), to contemporary issues, such as abortion or capital punishment, about which people of faith honestly disagree.

Many of us struggle with questions that may put us at odds with those whom we respect most—our parents, a beloved pastor, priest, rabbi, or valued friends—and we face the dilemma of balancing their wisdom and counsel with the integrity of our own understanding and belief.

Sometimes, we, too, feel, with Susan, that "I may believe it for church, but I'm not sure I *really* believe it."

Most of us have been taught that our faith/church/religion (whatever it may be) is the true one. If you are Jewish, your faith is based on the Law and the Prophets found in Jewish Scriptures and tradition. If you are Catholic, or a member of another creedally-based church, your faith reflects interpretations that have been a part of the church for centuries. If you come from a Protestant denomination that stresses the power of the pulpit and the authority of clergy to "preach the word," your personal faith will often reflect the interpretations, divinely inspired or otherwise, of those preachers who have most influenced you. The word "parson" is a derivative of "person," used in early Protestantism to indicate the education and wisdom of the clergyman who often *was* the most important person in the town; one who spoke with true authority.

Even those who belong to the so-called free churches, where freedom of personal conscience is extolled, usually have statements of faith to guide them. Although not necessarily binding upon the individual, they express "those things most commonly believed among us." So, whatever our tradition, most of us have been raised to believe that *its* expression of faith is God's expression of faith.

So, the pastor's response to Chuck or Susan presents a paradox: what is the appropriate balance between a faith tradition that has withstood the test of time and the need to help an individual find an interpretation that truly speaks to her or his individual needs? Different faith communities, and the wide variety of pastors within them, will deal with the paradox in different ways, as will all the Chucks and Susans of varying personality types and psychological attitudes, wherever they may be on their faith journeys.

It is not my purpose here to extol or promote questioning and doubt as somehow *better than* the acceptance of more traditional faith. However, in the light of emerging attitudes within an increasingly secular culture, we who are the leaders of today's churches *must* recognize that there are many people in our pews and, increasingly, far more *outside* the church who have genuine questions about matters of faith and belief that they do not feel are adequately answered by many churches. (One of the most striking, if disquieting findings of the FD/ALC study was the number of respondents who reported negative experiences related to their faith in the church. Although each story was different, the typical pattern revolved around being censured or admonished not to question when they came to clergy or other religious leaders with their concerns.)

Increasingly in our time, people's attitudes toward religious faith have been changing. There are many reasons for this, but among the most obvious and significant are *changing lifestyles* and the *knowledge explosion.*

The term "lifestyle" has come into our vocabulary within the lifetime of the baby boom generation. We see it in the mobility of people today. Most of us no longer are born, live, and die in the same community, or even in the same state, county, or province. Increasingly, people are on the move—corporate promotions, opportunities for new and different jobs, and retirement to warmer climes take most of us thousands of miles from a previous residence. Many of us make several such moves in a lifetime. The rapid increase of divorce has had repercussions in nearly every family. Changing sabbath attitudes have been accompanied by the proliferation of shopping malls and athletic events that impact our Saturday and Sunday habits. Contemporary people are faced with a multitude of new options for our dollar, time, and activities. Religion is no longer a central focus of the community; it is but *one option.* Faith, therefore, has become less a foundation than but one of many elements in peoples' lives.

The *explosion of knowledge* really hit our society following World War II and, with the development of the computer in more recent times, has proliferated far beyond anyone's expectations. The new knowledge of geology and astronomy force our rethinking of traditional biblical images. Some still debate the issues of evolution and creationism, but no longer is the church necessarily equated with the traditional position. New understandings of psychology and sociology help us understand people in far more complex ways than we did in earlier times. More of us have the opportunity for higher education, and the emerging role of continuing education has made the concept of "lifelong learning" a reality for all who wish to take advantage of it. Increasingly, the model of education has moved from one of "teacher orientation," with its emphasis on the transmission of tradition, to one of "learner orientation," with greater emphasis on the needs of the individual. Adults today must sort and choose, in their education and daily lives, from an increasing variety of options, and these patterns cannot help but affect their attitudes toward their faith.

Increasingly, contemporary men and women are faced with options of faith that of necessity lead to, at least, *some* questioning and doubt. Walt, in Chapter Two, is an example of one who has serious reservations about traditional approaches to religion, and is highly vocal about them in his church's study group. We encounter Walts in church every week, but they are still a minority—*most of the Walts have opted out of the church long ago.*

Leslie Weatherhead, an outstanding British clergyman of the mid-twentieth century, addressed some of the key issues of questioning and doubt in his provocative book, *The Christian Agnostic.* Identifying *himself* as a Christian agnostic, he clarifies the seeming paradox in the juxtaposition of the two terms by reminding the reader that an agnostic is not an atheist, who *denies* a belief in God, but rather one who has questions, who wants to get more information before making decisions of faith. Agnostics seek to learn from tradition, but ultimately must work out the answers of faith for themselves.

The term "Christian agnostic," according to Weatherhead, refers to

> ...a person who is immensely attracted by Christ and who seeks to show his spirit, to meet the challenges, hardships, and sorrows of life in the light of that spirit, but who, though he is sure of many Christian truths, feels he cannot honestly and conscientiously "sign on the dotted line" that he believes certain theological ideas about which some branches of the church dogmatize; churches from which he feels excluded because he cannot "believe." His intellectual integrity makes him say about many things, "it may be so. I do not know."[1]

Weatherhead says to the modern lay person:

> Don't exclude yourself from the fellowship of Christ's followers because of mental difficulties. If you love Christ and are seeking to follow him, take an attitude of Christian agnosticism to intellectual problems at least for the present.[2]

As a young pastor, I was greatly helped by Weatherhead's book when it was first published in 1965, and I made the decision to preach on the topic of "Christian Agnosticism." When the sermon title was announced, some eyebrows in the congregation were raised, and the church was very full that Sunday. However, after the service, the response was electric. "Now I know what I am," one man said to me at the church door. A woman expressed her appreciation for the concept: "It's the first time I've ever been told from the pulpit that it's all right to raise some questions about my faith." In the months and years that followed, 16 more sermons on beliefs, doctrines, and theological issues were preached "from the perspective of Christian agnosticism." The concept, even more than the phrase, struck a nerve where many people were, and they grew spiritually because they were encouraged to look at their faith with a critical and questioning eye.

Now, I'm not going to belabor the term any further, other than to urge those intrigued by the concept of Christian agnosticism to avail themselves of Weatherhead's book and read it. Its importance lies in its challenge to the contemporary church to take seriously those men and women who truly want to believe, to grow in faith, and to find meaning in the great heritage that religion has given them. However, they can do so only in the context of seeking, and finding, for themselves, answers to the eternal questions of the ages, not because of what others may say but as a result of the explorations along their own journeys of faith.

Traditionally, the late teens and early twenties is a time for questioning one's religious traditions and beliefs. Young men and women are disengaging from being children within their parents' family structures and striking out to establish their own adult lives. Part of this involves forming their own patterns of faith and belief that speak to their needs as they begin to take their own faithing seriously. Some do it by dropping out of the traditional church completely; others explore a wide variety of often offbeat cults and religious forms; for still others it is a process of ferment and change, both intellectual and emotional, that they must experience as a part of growing up. Too often, parents decry this transition, feeling their children have "lost the faith" when, in reality, they should be rejoicing that their son or daughter is truly maturing into a fullness of faith that is truly his or her own.

The spirit of questioning and doubting so identified with young adulthood is seen also throughout the life cycle. Chuck's statement that he is "asking questions now" that he never even thought of in his adolescence is increasingly a part of the so-called mature, adult years. The FD/ALC study found significant questioning about matters of faith among those in their late thirties and their forties. It works in both directions: some people for whom faith has seemed irrelevant find new positive meaning as they deal with their midlife transitions, while others who have been vigorous and active churchgoers for years find themselves increasingly on the fringe as they seek to deal with new questions and new issues in their lives.

Both Westerhoff and Fowler (discussed in Chapter Two) stress the importance of a questioning stance as *necessary* for growth in faith.

Westerhoff's concept of "Searching Faith" stresses the roles of doubt and/or critical judgment. Here I reiterate and amplify a quotation made earlier:

> In order to move from an understanding of faith that belongs to the community to an understanding of faith that is our own, we need to doubt and question that faith. At this point, "religion of the head" becomes equally important with the "religion of the heart...."[3]

Fowler's Stage 4, "Individuative-Reflective" (subtitled "The Critic" by McCollough) also stresses dealing with one's own faith questions and issues at this point in the faith development process:

> For a genuine move to Stage 4 to occur there must be an inter-ruption of reliance on external sources of authority. The "tyr-anny of the they"—or the potential for it—must be under-mined.[4]

The FD/ALC study also affirms the importance, even necessity, of some period of reflection, questioning, doubt, and—even more—rethinking and rebuilding one's faith structures if people are truly to mature in their faith. This research emphasizes the important role the church can play in helping people through this important, but often dif-ficult, period in their faith lives. The community of faith that nurtures and encourages individual expressions of personal faith, *even when they may digress from established norms,* must be affirmed. That parish, syna-gogue, or congregation that rejoices in diversity and sees the sharing of different faith understandings as an indication of both individual and corporate faithing is clearly encouraging spiritual growth.

That community of faith that encourages such spiritual growth is being faithful to a basic principle of adult learning (adult faithing): that mature persons ultimately must work through for themselves that which will have true meaning for their lives. For some, this may mean the rejection of some early religious training or traditional con-cepts, something our culture has historically viewed as negative. However, the positive results in the spiritual development of individ-uals make it worth the effort.

Consider this analogy. On her birthday, you can give your daugh-ter an expensive, intricately constructed toy that is programmed to do a variety of things. All she has to do is plug it in or wind it up, press a button, or move a lever. The toy itself does everything, and she "participates" by, essentially, *watching* it happen. And, in time, she will tire of it.

Or, you can give her a creative toy—the pieces of a puzzle, the building blocks with which she can build a house, a boat, an auto, or a "something" out of her own imaginative mind. With these basic pieces, she can create something of pleasure that is wholly hers in the fullest sense of the term. How much better for her development is the latter than the former.

In matters of faith, you can give her a creed, a tradition, and a denomination and say "These are your faith—do not question them!" They are a total package, and her response will be the result of many factors as she matures. She may adhere to your teachings without question or, in later years, she may well reject it all.

Or, you can help her to think, and to worship, to study, to pray—all building blocks of faith—but say to her: "These are the basic *components* of your faith, but you must put them together in those ways *that have meaning for you*. You must create your own creed. Your faith must be *your own* response to those options you have considered." This alternative is, for me, the ultimate goal of the faithing experience.

The words of the Buddha are germane here:

> Believe nothing because a so-called wise man said it.
> Believe nothing because a belief is generally held.
> Believe nothing because it is written in ancient books.
> Believe nothing because it is said to be of divine origin.
> Believe nothing because someone else believes it.
> Believe only what you yourself judge to be true.[5]

The thrust of this chapter has moved counter to many traditional understandings of faith. I hope that, for some readers, it will stimulate consideration of some refreshing and different perspectives. That alone will make the emphasis worthwhile.

Of far greater importance, however, are the implications of this emphasis on the *positive* role of questioning and some healthy doubt in faith development. For the synagogue, congregation, or parish, it suggests that our primary task is still, and always will be, to affirm our historic faith and traditions, to teach them and assume them as basic to the faith of every member and active participant. However, beyond that, the community of faith—clergy and laity alike—must also recognize the difficulty that some have with tradition and help them to deal with it constructively. This does not necessarily mean that the church glibly says "Believe whatever you want." Rather, the truly vital community of faith will help its people explore the options and possibilities, and discover for themselves those answers to their questions that will help them find the fullest possible personal faith for their lives. Affirm the searching: "I'm glad you're asking those questions. They are important. Let's explore them together."

For the reader who does have questions, you are not alone. You don't need to apologize: "I know I ought to believe in (whatever), but...." Rather, speak honestly, "I have some real questions that I want to deal with. For example...." Respect the tradition of the faith community and the beliefs of others, but continue to press until they have meaning *for you.*

The words of Scripture are very true: "Seek, and you will find."

For Reflection

1. Why do so many people view questioning and doubt about matters of faith as negative? Why are some people unwilling (or unable) to raise questions about matters of faith?

2. How do you react to the concept of "Christian agnosticism" as suggested by Leslie Weatherhead? How is it helpful? If it bothers you, why? What would you suggest as a better term?

3. Both Westerhoff and Fowler's theories of faith development involve the necessity of all persons going through some period in their lives in which the questioning attitude predominates if they are truly to mature in their faith. Do you agree with this? Why? Why not? Is it possible for a person to become truly mature in his or her faith *without* any significant questioning or doubt (i.e. moving directly from Fowler's Stage 3 to Stage 5)?

4. In the context of the community of faith, what can we say to people like Walt?

CHAPTER FOUR

"VIVE LA DIFFERENCE!"

*Gender Differences
in the Faithing Process*

THE FRENCH HAVE A PHRASE FOR IT. With a reputation (rightly or wrongly) for placing high values on the physical, intellectual, and social relationships between men and women, they proclaim with joy, "Vive la difference!" In a time when sexual equality is highly valued and emerging social patterns tend to blur the differences between sexes, the phrase reminds us that there *is* a social and physical dynamic between men and women that enriches all concerned. In terms of faith development, I echo the words of a colleague at a meeting committed to the equality of women in the church, who said, "I'd still like to find a theologically inclusive statement of 'vive la difference!' "

Tom and Helen have been married for 23 years. They have three children, all in some phase of moving out of the family nest. For the most part, their marriage is a happy one. Yet, in the past few years, they've both become aware that they have had an increasing number of "strong discussions" (not quite arguments) about issues that, in one way or another, ultimately relate to matters of faith. Helen needles Tom that his interest in church attendance has waned since the children grew up. Tom has been thinking a good bit about the question of what follows death. He's told Helen he wants to be cremated when his time comes, and this has been a shock to her, since her beliefs about death and the afterlife totally reject cremation as a possibility. She'd like for the two of them to discuss it with their pastor, but Tom will have nothing of it. "That's a matter for me to decide!" he states firmly every time the question is raised. And so it goes.

Some of the differences between men and women in matters of faith, as symbolized by Tom and Helen's faith discussions, can be attributed simply to religious upbringing—the families and the churches each grew up in. Some of the differences may be primarily extensions of their own separate personalities. This is particularly true after the children are gone. The "glue" of "what's best for the children," which previously provided a common stance for father and mother, is no longer there. Increasingly, each spouse's emerging interests and individual identity erode common purposes and values.

However, another important factor cannot be dismissed. Quite simply, there seem to be some basic differences between men and women in the ways they approach life in general and faith-issues in particular. The matter of gender differences has become a topic of increased study and interest in the social sciences, but only recently has it begun to be addressed in the context of faith development.

When we began the FD/ALC study in 1981, I was struck by the number of people who asked if women would be a part of the sample studied. Frankly, the question surprised me, since we had never considered doing anything that did not involve *both* women and men. However, the questions were not unfounded, since several major studies in human development have limited their inquiry to men, but have tended to generalize for the total population. This concern, plus a recognition of the changing roles of men and women today, led us to establish the study's first hypothesis:

> The dynamics of *faith development* are different for men and women.

A hypothesis is a statement that may or may not be true. Stating it one way or another does not necessarily suggest what the researchers *hope* they will find. The study had seven hypotheses. Some were affirmed, some were not, while in others the findings were ambiguous. Our purpose with this hypothesis , however, was to explore what differences between men's and women's approaches to matters of faith did appear.

First, let's look at some of the similarities between men and women related to faith development. We found many on the basis of our interviews. Among them were:

•Men and women are equally likely to believe that faith should change over the life span. We asked whether or not the person felt comfortable with the idea of a person's faith changing just as the body and mind change as one matures. Both men and women responded positively in a two-to-one ratio over the negative response. Both women and men appear to affirm the concept of growth and development of faith through the life cycle.

Believe Faith Should Change	Men	Women
Yes	66%	64%
No	32%	32%
No answer	2%	4%
Total	100%	100%

•Men and women express similar patterns of faith change since adolescence. The women's percentages were a bit higher than men's in stating that they had "more faith now than at age 16" and, interestingly, "less faith now than at age 16," while the figures tipped the other way slightly with more men than women indicating "no change." All in all, however, there is really no significant difference between these responses based on gender.

Change in Faith Index	Men	Women
More faith than at age 16	53%	54%
No change	32%	29%
Less faith than at age 16	15%	17%
Total	100%	100%

•In Module 2, each of the 41 persons interviewed was evaluated in terms of his or her faith stage, using the Fowler structure. We found little significant difference in patterns of faith development, i.e., men and women tend to move through the stages in similar ways. There is no indication of any major differences between the proportion of women and men in each stage, or at what ages they tend to be in each stage, or how rapidly they got there.

In summary, we found a high degree of similarity between the faith journeys of men and women through adulthood. Some of the *differences,* however, were intriguing.

Most of the differences revolve around the ways men and women *experience* faith. If we could find little difference in the nature of beliefs and faith attitudes held, there certainly were several to be found in terms of faith experience.

•Some important life experiences affect men and women in significantly different ways. It is not so much the experience itself, but the way it affects the individual, and the way he or she functions. It would appear that there are life experiences that motivate women far more than men with respect to raising questions about faith and life's meaning. Among the most significant are the following:

> —The same proportion of men and women report having dealt with the death of a loved one, but women are more likely than men to report that this experience affected their thinking about the meaning and purpose of life in a significant way.
> —Among those who report a "born-again" experience, women are more likely than men to report that it affected their thoughts about the meaning of life a great deal.
> —Another event of importance for women in turning their thoughts to the meaning of life is considering an abortion (whether for themselves or for another). Nearly 60% who considered an abortion report it affected their thoughts a great deal, compared with fewer than 40% among men.

It would appear, therefore, that women reflect upon the emotional and spiritual overtones of important life experiences more than do men. This is neither positive nor negative in itself, but it does suggest one of the important differences in the way the two sexes relate personal experience to their own faith.

Life Event	Proportion of total who had the experience:	Proportion of these who report that the experience had affected their thoughts and feelings a great deal:
Death of a Loved One:		
Men	86%	51%
Women	85%	65%
Born-Again Experience:		
Men	28%	75%
Women	35%	84%
Considered an Abortion for Self or Another:		
Men	12%	38%
Women	15%	57%

•Women and men differ significantly in terms of the kind of support they seek when faced with an important problem. In the survey we posed this question:

During your lifetime, have you ever:

Received a promotion or honor at work?
Had a baby (as father or mother)?
Had a divorce?
Experienced the death of a loved one?
Been lonely for a long period of time?
Had a "born again" experience?
Been seriously worried about your health?
Been out of work for a long period of time?
Considered an abortion for yourself or someone close to you?
Made a conscious decision to leave a church or religious group?
Received counseling for emotional difficulty?

The percentages ranged from 86% ("Experienced the death of a loved one") to 13% ("Considered an abortion...") and there was little significant percentage difference between male and female responses.

When we asked a question about how this affected their thoughts about the meaning and purpose of life, however, in three of them the male and female responses were significantly different. These three have been reported in the section above.

However, we then posed a *follow-up* question that sought to find out how they *dealt* with these life problems. The responses are intriguing and significant. Here is the question and the summary of responses.

When you are faced with a problem or crisis, like those in the previous question, to which of the following kinds of support would you likely turn for help?

	All Respondents	Men	Women
Share it with family.	87%	86%	88%
Share it with close friends.	73%	69%	77%
Discuss it with a class or group in your church or synagogue.	23%	17%	27%
Work it through on your own.	80%	85%	75%
Read the Bible or other inspirational literature.	64%	56%	72%
Seek help from a religious counselor.	40%	35%	46%
Seek other professional counseling.	31%	28%	34%
Seek help from a support group.	26%	22%	29%
Pray about it.	80%	74%	86%

These responses suggest a striking difference between men and women. As you can see, in eight categories women had a higher percentage response than did men. Each of *these* categories involved looking beyond themselves for help, whether to other individuals (family, friends, counselors), groups (class, support group), divine guidance (prayer), or reading (Bible, inspirational literature). In only one category, "Work it through on your own," was the male percentage response higher than that of the female.

These differences are further underscored by the responses of men and women to another question posed in the Module 1 survey. In an effort to get some idea of how different people define "faith," we asked:

"Which one of the following four statements comes closest to your own view of 'faith'?":

> A set of beliefs
> Membership in a church or synagogue
> Finding meaning in life
> A relationship with God

Significantly more women than men chose "A relationship with God," while significantly more men than women opted for "A set of beliefs." Gender differences on the other two statements were not statistically significant:

	All Respondents	Men	Women
A relationship with God	51%	44%	57%
Finding meaning in life	20%	21%	19%
A set of beliefs	19%	24%	15%
Membership in a church or synagogue	4%	3%	5%
(Concept not meaningful)	1%	2%	1%
No opinion	5%	6%	3%
	100%	100%	100%

What does this mean? The most plausible interpretation is that women are more "relational" and "social" in matters of faith and life issues than are men; they feel more comfortable sharing their beliefs as well as their problems about personal matters with others than do their male counterparts. Men, conversely, tend to be more structured in their religious beliefs and to keep their attitudes and feelings about matters of faith and life more closely within themselves. They "hold their cards close to the vest," so to speak. For men, one's faith seems to be a very private matter to a greater degree than to women.

•In another question, we asked all respondents how much they had *thought about* each of the following subjects. Here is how they responded:

Proportion giving much thought to...	Men	Women
Living a worthwile life	61%	72%
Your relation to God	51%	66%
Basic meaning and value of life	52%	64%
Developing your faith	37%	57%

In every case, the positive response from women was higher than that of men, all the percentage differences being statistically significant. The greatest difference dealt with the question of "Developing your faith," in which more than half of the women, but only about a third of the men indicated that this was a matter about which they had given much thought.

•Women also differ from men in the degree to which they attach importance to religion. Again, a majority of women compared with only about four men in ten report that religion is very important in their lives. By an even greater margin, women are more likely than men to see religion as a *positive experience* in their lives.

•Women are more likely than are men to report the belief that life is meaningful or has a purpose.

	Men	Women
Believe religion is very important	42%	56%
Believe religion is a very positive experience	29%	47%
Believe that life has meaning and purpose is very important	63%	76%

•In Module 2, our face-to-face interview research, we were able to do some other analyses, based on Fowler's stages of faith development (cf. Chapter Two). Perhaps the most important finding, in terms of male/female differences, was that women have a harder time than do men in moving from Stage 3 into Stage 4, and an easier time than men in moving from Stage 4 to Stage 5. Men, however, tend to stay in Stage 4 longer than do women.

This would suggest that women feel more comfortable in Stage 3, with its emphasis on conforming to the values of one's social group, and have some real difficulty moving into Stage 4, with its strong emphasis on individualism. We have already seen these factors illustrated in other responses noted above. The role expectations in our society have traditionally put greater expectations for independent thinking and action upon men and the qualities of socialization and relationships upon women. Although these patterns are currently changing (and will be addressed shortly), research cannot help but reflect patterns of living that have been an integral part of the lives of those interviewed.

Similarly, the seemingly greater desire of women for fuller dimensions of the faithing experience apparently motivate their more rapid movement from Stage 4 to Stage 5. Conversely, men tend to be more reticent to give up Stage 4's more tentative and questioning stance.

•Finally, a striking difference between women and men comes from Module 2's psychosocial analysis. It is based on the work of Erik Erikson, the well-known psychologist. Erikson's theory of human development involves a series of polarities throughout life between positive and negative psychological and social (psychosocial) responses to life's problems and crises. (See Chapter Five.) The persons interviewed were evaluated in terms of the ways they dealt with these crisis experiences, utilizing the Erikson framework.

Put simply, the men in the sample had almost *three times* as many unresolved or negatively resolved psychosocial polarities as did the women interviewed. These dealt mainly with issues of trust vs. mistrust, identity vs. identity confusion, and intimacy vs. isolation. Significantly more men tended toward the negative resolution of each than did women. This does not necessarily imply that men are less balanced psychologically than are women. It does suggest, however, that men appear to deal with issues of faith and life more individually and less socially than do women, and illustrates further what has been seen throughout this summary of the research findings: there *are* significant differences between the ways women and men *experience* their faith.

Before reflecting a bit on the meaning of these findings, we must address a very real question that has been asked by many: *Are these differences based primarily on the biological differences between men and women, or are they really factors of cultural upbringing and religious socialization that have given men and women certain role expectations that are reflected in the research findings?*

We have no way of knowing for sure, at least from the FD/ALC

study, but most of the other research focusing on gender differences
would suggest that distinctions between men and women are partially
due to physical differences, *but much more* tied to cultural patterns. In
light of the rapidly changing roles played by men and women today,
it would be interesting to do a similar survey in another 10 years to
see if the research results were different. However, for the moment,
we must utilize the findings we have from this first major study of its
type, and reflect upon its meaning for our own faithing.

Some Trends

As has been noted, the FD/ALC research reflects responses in 1985.
Concurrently, a major restructuring of our society's image of appropriate roles for men and women is taking place. Too often, reports on
the "feminist movement" are skewed to emphasize unfortunately bizarre aspects at both ends of the spectrum. Far too much emphasis has
been put on unisex bathrooms in the marketplace or God-as-female in
the church. Of greater importance, significant changes for the better
are taking place in which a more equal and creatively dynamic relationship between the sexes is emerging. In light of this trend in our
culture, we briefly suggest several implications for the faith development of individuals and, therefore, for the parish, synagogue, or congregation that seeks to minister to those individuals.

Women's professional roles in the church are changing
rapidly and significantly.
Probably the most obvious change has come with the large numbers of
women ordained in many Christian and Jewish bodies in the last generation, and the significant ferment around the issue among Catholics. Unfortunately, there is still resistance within many denominations and local
congregations that have put limitations on the kinds of ministries wom-
en can perform, but this is changing and the professional role for women
clergy is being defined in new, creative, and exciting ways. Certainly the
concept of team ministries, sometimes with one's ordained spouse, is
producing a whole host of new possibilities utilizing the best of the qualities of both femininity and masculinity in pastoral leadership.

The role of non-ordained women in the church is also changing.
It used to be that men were on the boards and committees making the
decisions for the congregation. The women were in the kitchen mak-

ing coffee, or in the classroom teaching the children. Now, in most contemporary churches, these patterns are changing markedly. Women serve as presidents of congregations and fathers (or grandfathers) are leaders in the pre-school class. This change is for the best in the eyes of many, if not most, people but it is still a threat to others. Texts in the Bible are still interpreted, by some, to prescribe the "place of women" in the church, and even some women find themselves a bit uncomfortable with their new roles. But the roles *are* changing and it will be interesting to see what new patterns of church participation may occur. Some fear that, with leadership roles changing, fewer men will remain active in the church. Others look to a dynamic in which both women and men find new, creative, and more meaningful ways of participating in the corporate faithing experience. Let us hope for and work for the latter.

A new emphasis on family ministry is emerging.

As we become increasingly aware of the roles played by *both* husband and wife in the raising of children, the church must affirm and undergird this dual responsibility. It takes a variety of forms, from the requirement that both parents participate in the preparation for a child's baptism, to team teaching in the educational program, to provision for experiences of family worship, both in the church and in the home.

Children also need to be helped to understand their integral role in the family faithing experience. We talk often about how parents teach the child, but oftentimes forget that we parents are also learning from our children. Mrs. Anna, in *The King and I*, hired to teach the king's many children, begins a song with these words:

> It's a very ancient saying
> But a true and honest thought,
> That if you become a teacher,
> By your pupils you'll be taught.

How many of us parents, in a fit of temper, have punished a child unfairly, and perhaps said things we're sorry for later. Bedtime comes, and as we are tucking the little one in, the simple words come forth, "I love you, daddy." Who is teaching whom?

Ministry to those of different sexual orientations.

As we recognize the role of families and rejoice in the creative diversity of the genders, we are also profoundly aware of a lifestyle that has always been with us, but only in recent years has come into the open—that of gay and lesbian sexual orientation. Few issues are as sensitive as this one, and I mention it only in passing to assure that it is not overlooked. What is important is that, for many adults—probably more than most of us think—this dimension of sexual orientation is an integral part of their ego images and, therefore, of their faith development. A young man questions a God who would "do this to me." Two middle-aged women living together leave a church because of the "speculation" about them within the congregation. A young woman suffers doubly, as her divorce is based on her liaison with another woman. Two young men wish to join a congregation and have their new member picture taken together; membership is not denied, but having their pictures *taken together* is. Isolated incidents? Perhaps, but they clearly illustrate two things: one's sexuality, straight or gay, *does* play a part in one's faith development. These kinds of issues are increasingly being faced by the community of faith, and must be dealt with sensitively and lovingly for all concerned.

Male/female differences are an aid to faithing.
As leaders and participants become more sensitive to some of the gender differences suggested in this chapter, it cannot help but enrich the dynamic of adult classes, study, and support groups. Men-only or women-only groupings are often best for some situations and topics, and the mixed group, particularly where there is discussion and interaction, provides a different but important dynamic. Whenever I ask a large gathering to form small groups for conversation, I stress having *both* men and women in each circle whenever possible. The discussion is invariably richer because of the male and female perspectives involved.

We need to be able to share our faith stories with others.
The finding that men particularly have difficulty with the resolution of psychosocial issues, and with moving from Stage 4 to Stage 5, discussed earlier in the chapter, suggests that we need to be more sensitive in giving people the opportunity to deal with life and faith issues. Somehow, we need to provide new and non-threatening ways for men and women alike to talk together at a more intimate and meaningful level because of the different perceptions they bring to the faith journey. In response to FD/ALC Module 2 interviews, which involved reflecting upon and sharing with another one's faith story, many of

those interviewed stated that this was the first time they had ever been encouraged to reflect upon their own journey of faith. Several, when asked about the opportunity for this in their church, just laughed and said, "Never."

As we as individuals come to understand ourselves more fully and see our faith in the context of our adult development, we will each mature spiritually. The more we can do so in the context of a loving and supportive community of faith, the church will be stronger and its people more active in their faithing. One of the central ingredients comes from our understanding and affirmation of the significant contributions men and women can make to each other in this faithing process. Men may need to learn to be more open in sharing their faith stories; women may need to be more assertive about breaking some of the traditional molds in the church. As these things happen, all benefit.

"Male and female He created them" (Genesis 1:27). The masculine in all of us and the feminine in all of us, working together, bring out the best in all of us. *Vive la difference!*

For Reflection

1. To what extent and in what ways do these findings reflect cultural stereotypes regarding men and women? Should we affirm and build upon them or seek to change them? Why? How?
2. In what ways do the similarities and differences between men and women discussed in this chapter suggest helpful ways for you in your personal faithing? In your relationship with your spouse? In the mixed study/discussion group in your parish, congregation, or synagogue?
3. What do these findings suggest to our traditionally male-dominated religious structures? To what extent and in what ways are these religious structures changing because of the emerging new roles of women in contemporary secular society?
4. In the light of these findings, what are the strengths/weaknesses of class/study groups/retreats in the church that are for men or women only? For mixed groups?

CHAPTER FIVE

"A TIME TO BE BORN, A TIME TO DIE"

Faithing Through the Adult Life Cycle

MY WIFE AND TEN OTHER WOMEN once held a birthday party for a good friend. What made this party different was that these "friends" woke her up singing "Happy Birthday" outside her bedroom window *at 6:00* A.M. What a birthday greeting! Why? Well, it was Marjean's 40th birthday...a very special milepost in her life...and it couldn't be just an *ordinary* party!

I remember flying from the west coast back to Minnesota on my fifty-fifth birthday. I hadn't thought much about my birthday until I got off the plane and was greeted by my wife, two sons, and a daughter-in-law with six helium-filled balloons and a gigantic sign proclaiming "Happy 55th Birthday, Ken/Dad. You are now a *junior*-senior citizen!"

Why all the hoopla? I don't remember adults acting this way when I was younger. Maybe they did, but my image was that even those special birthdays were celebrated with proper decorum: ice cream and cake, and a few appropriate gifts. People have moved through the adult life cycle since the beginning of time, but today we seem to be more aware of and more sensitive to the aging process than ever before. In *As You Like It*, Shakespeare reminds us of life's inevitable scenario:

> All the world's a stage,
> And all the men and women merely players:
> They have their exits and entrances;
> And one man in his time plays many parts,
> His acts being seven ages. At first the infant,
> Mewling and puking in the nurse's arms.
> And then the whining school-boy, with his satchel
> And shining morning face, creeping like snail
> Unwillingly to school. And then the lover,
> Sighing like furnace, with a woeful ballad
> Made to his mistress' eyebrow. Then a soldier,
> Full of strange oaths and bearded like the pard,
> Jealous in honour, sudden and quick in quarrel,
> Seeking the bubble reputation
> Even in the cannon's mouth. And then the justice,
> In fair round belly with good capon lined.
> With eyes severe and beard of formal cut,
> Full of wise saws and modern instances;
> And so he plays his part. The sixth age shifts
> Into the lean and slipper'd pantaloon,
> With spectacles on nose and pouch on side,
> His youthful hose, well saved, a world too wide
> For his shrunk shank; and his big manly voice,
> Turning again toward childish treble, pipes
> And whistles in his sound. Last scene of all,
> That ends with strange eventful history,
> Is second childishness and mere oblivion,
> Sans teeth, sans eyes, sans taste, sans everything.[1]

The contrast between Shakespeare's somber view of the human life cycle and today's almost nervous-humored approach is symbolic of our culture's changing attitude toward aging. In earlier times, the individual had little control of the process; now there are many things we can do and do do to find the fullest meaning in life. Times have changed and our attitudes have become more positive and creative, with those well into today's sixth or seventh ages jogging five miles a day, jetting from continent to continent on an AARP tour, or studying world politics in an Elderhostel course. Ashley Montague said it well with his statement: "I'm going to die young...*as late in life as possible!*"

Because we now better understand some of the ways we develop throughout the life cycle and are able to control at least some of the process, we are today better able to laugh at the foibles of aging. A group of Colorado skiers can call themselves the "Over the Hill Gang," and we all can chuckle about our bloopers with the explanation that "I'm going through my midlife crisis."

After I had used some tongue-in-cheek humor like this in a presentation to a local church adult group, one woman approached me and asked pointedly: "How can you joke about growing older? I can't." I wasn't sure whether she was chiding or praising me (and still am not), but my only answer was deadly serious: "There's nothing we can do about getting older, but there *is* something we can do about how we deal with it. For me, being able to laugh along the way keeps everything in perspective."

Although scholars have studied human development for several generations, the popular interest in the *adult* life cycle probably had its springboard with the publication of Gail Sheehy's *Passages* in the late 1970s. Mixing current research with real-life stories written in a personal and salty style, the life structures of *Passages* were the kind with which the average person could identify.

But it was more than just a popular book. Adult life styles *are* changing. With fewer children and a lengthened life span, the so-called "middle years" have more than doubled. Many North American and European adults today have both the discretionary time and the financial resources necessary to develop themselves through a variety of experiences that were just not possible for their parents or grandparents. The intrigue of the life cycle comes as one of the by-products of a changing culture. Each season of life has its own meaning and opportunity, and contemporary adults are learning to savor each to the fullest.

Obviously, development has been fundamental to human life from the beginning: a child is born; he or she grows and matures physically, mentally, and socially through the unique interaction of genetic and environmental factors in childhood, adolescence, maturity, and old age to death. Although this development was not studied scientifically for centuries, it *happened*, perhaps not too differently than it does now, as human beings "did what comes naturally."

It was not until the twentieth century, as a part of the emerging disciplines of the social sciences, that scholars looked seriously at the phenomenon of the human life cycle, and the field of developmental psychology began to emerge. Until about mid-century, most developmental studies focused on children, later expanding into adolescence. Apparently, development took place until the late teens, after which adults pretty much made it on their own. Stephen R. Graubard, in his preface to *Adulthood*, edited by developmentalist Erik Erikson, puts it succinctly:

> Adults in contemporary society are still generally viewed in too undifferentiated a manner; all too little thought is given to the ways in which they differ from one another or from children. Despite the growth of interest in the human life cycle, we still know far too little about the "stages" of adult life, not nearly enough about the transition from adolescence to adulthood, and surprisingly little about middle age, let alone senescence.[2]

A generation later, Roger Gould, writing in the 1970s, makes a similar affirmation with delightful whimsy:

> Like a butterfly, an adult is supposed to emerge fully formed and on cue after a succession of developmental stages of childhood....Equipped with...wisdom and rationality, the adult supposedly remains quiescent for another half century or so. While children change, adults only age.[3]

However, these perceptions are changing rapidly. In the late 1940s, educator Robert Havighurst, in his *Developmental Tasks and Education* was probably the first social scientist to look at the *entire* life cycle. He suggests that, in each period of life, an individual has to face and deal with specific *tasks* that are a part of her or his developmental needs at that time. He calls these "developmental tasks." So, the toddler must learn to walk and talk, and the six year old must cope with beginning school, and the adolescent begins to mature and works at finding his or her own identity outside the family role. Similarly *young adults* must establish themselves vocationally and, for most, select a mate and begin a family. Developmental tasks of *middle age* range from relating to one's spouse as a person after the children are gone to new relationships with aging parents. *Later maturity* means adjusting to retirement, perhaps the death of a spouse, and decreasing physical strength and health. With his simple concept of "developmental tasks," Havighurst helped us begin to understand something of the nature of human development over the *entire* life span.

At about the same time, Erikson, a psychologist, was also developing his own structure of human development, again including adults. Ultimately, Erikson's theory became more widely known than Havighurst's, and has provided much of the foundation for further developmental research during the generation that followed his *Childhood and Society*, first published in 1950.

Erikson's theory suggests that human personality evolves in eight stages over the life span, each of which produces a crisis, or turning point, in the form of a conflict between alternative attitudes. For each of these periods, Erikson sets forth criteria of relative psychosocial health with a tension between the favorable (positive) and unfavorable (negative) polarities of that tension. The degree to which each individual resolves these polarities positively (or negatively) provides an important basis for her or his personality.

Although Erikson's eight stages are all in operation, to some degree, *throughout life*, each is especially important during a particular period of the life cycle. The stages and normal periods of ascendancy, plus the positive and negative attributes associated with them, are as follows:

Stage	Period	Favorable Resolution	Unfavorable Resolution
1	Early Infancy	Trust	Mistrust
2	Late Infancy	Autonomy	Shame and Doubt
3	Early Childhood	Initiative	Guilt
4	Middle Childhood	Industry	Inferiority
5	Adolescence	Identity	Identity Confusion
6	Young Adulthood	Intimacy	Isolation
7	Middle Adulthood	Generativity	Stagnation
8	Older Adulthood	Ego Integrity	Despair

Since our focus is on adults, the three stages commonly associated with adulthood are developed a bit more fully:

Intimacy vs Isolation (Young Adulthood)
One needs to establish a relationship(s) (not necessarily sexual) with one or more other person(s), usually approximately the same age, at a level of *intimacy* in which meaningful sharing can take place. When this does not happen the individual moves into psychosocial *isolation*.

Generativity vs Stagnation (Middle Adulthood)
Generativity is the concern for making this a better world for the next generation and actively working to contribute to this improvement. *Stagnation* represents the absence of this kind of involvement and caring, and a sense of purposelessness.

Ego Integrity vs Despair (Later Adulthood)
Ego integrity (Integration) involves looking back over one's life and feeling satisfied that it has had meaning. When one's life reflection is negative and filled with frustration, one must face life's end with a sense of *despair*.

Whereas Havighurst focuses on specific tasks, Erikson sees a broader range of dynamics ever in flux which, in particular, gives a fullness of dimension to adult life. The contribution of each of these pioneers to the field is significant.

In more recent times, Daniel Levinson's research on males in the 1970s has become highly regarded. In *The Seasons of a Man's Life*, Levinson sees an alternation between periods of relative *stability*, in which the man works primarily to build upon and improve existing life structures (work, family, friendships, etc.), and periods of *transition* when life patterns change and restructuring is needed (divorce, job change, move to a new community, etc.). He sees these periods alternating throughout the life cycle.

Levinson is now pursuing a comparable study of women. He indicates that there are many similarities but still quite a few differences between the male and female patterns of adult development. This companion volume will markedly enrich the already significant contribution Levinson has made to the field of adult development.

As has already been suggested, no contemporary statement about stages of adult development can overlook Gail Sheehy's *Passages*. She uses the decades to delineate her stages, with pithy titles for each, such as "The Trying Twenties," "The Catch Thirties," and "The Deadline Decade" (Forties) to capture an identity for each of these periods of life. She also provides a colorful analogy of how life transitions occur:

> We are not unlike a particularly hardy crustacean. The lobster grows by developing and shedding a series of hard, protective shells. Each time it expands from within, the confining shell must be sloughed off. It is left exposed and vulnerable until, in time, a new covering grows to replace the old.
>
> With each passage from one stage of human growth to the next, we, too, must shed a protective structure. We are left exposed and vulnerable—but also yeasty and embryonic again, capable of stretching in ways we hadn't known before.[4]

The authors we have looked at briefly (all too briefly, I am sure) are probably the best known in the field of adult development. However, other studies have been generated over the past 30 to 40 years as well. This work has been taking place during essentially the same time that the concepts of *faith development* (cf. Chapter Two) have been emerging. In a conversation with Daniel Levinson in 1980, I asked what he had learned about the faith dimension of adult development in *The Seasons of a Man's Life*. He reported that he had found little connection between the two in his research, but was intrigued with the concept—which, at the time, was new to him—and urged our group of religious educators to do something about it. Thus began the Faith Development in the Adult Life Cycle Project.

The FD/ALC study has been described in the Preface. Suffice it here to say that its fundamental purpose was to address the question of what relationships, if any, can be identified between aging and development throughout adulthood and the changes that may or may not take place in an individual's *faith* structures. Those who generated and supported the study wondered, for example, if there *were* patterns of alternation between periods of stability and periods of transition, such as Levinson had suggested for the male life cycle, in the development of one's faith. To be more specific, could we predict that faith development takes place at certain ages or periods throughout adulthood? We set out to find some of the answers.

Our major finding was that there is *not* a predictable pattern. However, there are some exceptions, and it is these exceptions that are significant.

Little was found to suggest any predictable clustering of faith change or development *based on chronology alone* throughout the adult life cycle. The study found that faith change/development occurs at *all* ages in adulthood and is determined by a wide variety of factors. It is apparent that faith development is influenced much more by the social context in which a person lives than by that person's age.

Two exceptions were apparent in the research, however, and a third was suggested. These tend to focus around three periods in the life span that emphasize transition. The two that were most clearly seen in the data relate to *young adulthood* and *midlife*.

The period of the late teens and early twenties is the time when the child is becoming an adult. When my son got his own apartment at nineteen, he was on his own, but only a few days passed before he was back at our house to see what was in the refrigerator or to do his laundry in our washer. When I asked him if they didn't have a laundromat at his apartment, he replied: "Yes, but that costs money!" He wasn't yet quite out of the nest. However, as the weeks and months went by, we saw him less and less often. He was making the transition from adolescence to adulthood.

This time of disengagement from one's parental home and the establishment of one's own identity in the adult community often also includes some rejection or modification of previous religious and values orientations. It may also involve acceptance, at least tentatively, of some new and perhaps very different philosophical and theological life perspectives. It is a time for asking questions and exploring new possibilities of faith expression. There are many Stage 4s (Fowler) involved in a Searching Faith (Westerhoff) during this period in one's life. Not only our research, but other studies, plus the experience of parents and churches alike, all attest that *young adulthood* is a time in which the ferment of changing, and often growing, faith attitudes is often quite pronounced.

The other exception, seen rather clearly in the FD/ALC data, points to some significant faithing—i.e. dealing with issues of one's faith— during the *midlife* period. Module 2 indicates increased psychosocial tension in the period between 36 and 45 years of age. This is not always seen as a crisis of faith, per se, but is probably focused around those struggles for meaning that often characterize the "midlife crisis." However, Module 2 also shows a continuing positive relationship between the resolution of psychosocial tensions and faith development. Therefore, it seems apparent that midlife—a critical time during which basic presuppositions are rethought, some discarded, and others restructured in the process of trying to make sense of life's meaning and purpose—*may well be a most crucial period of adult faith development*. At midlife, one rethinks many aspects of her or his life. One considers new vocational directions and, with the children growing out of their lives, married couples are usually dealing with the restructuring of their relationship. A variety of options, both professional and personal, force most of us to re-examine our lives to date and set new goals and directions for the future. The study found that, although people are not always consciously aware of the faithing that is going on in their lives, it does appear to be happening to a significant number of us.

There is also indication in the research that the years immediately before and after *retirement* appear also to be times of particular reflection upon some of life's ultimate values. As a person leaves the work force, he or she must deal with some significant loss of identity that had previously been defined by one's work—"I am a teacher," "I am a secretary," "I am an executive." Those of us fortunate enough to be in professions that can slowly diminish over the years—artists, consultants, and the like—may not always be aware of the profound sense of loss often felt by those for whom retirement is precise and immediate. To this end, Evelyn and James Whitehead in their book, *Christian Life Patterns*, suggest an important *spiritual* need for the retirement years: *to rejoice in one's "uselessness."* Yes, you read that right: "use*less*ness." Their point is:

> One does not depend on such things as social status, salary, or credentials to guarantee one's relationship with God. Yet despite the best insights of many religious traditions, societies and cultures insidiously convince us that it is by our usefulness that we are to be judged and are to judge ourselves.
>
> The religious critique of this "worldly" attitude...often takes the form of an emphasis on emptying.... The point here is that the event of retirement performs this very act. It empties out of a person's life perhaps the most sturdy crutch of self-worth, one's social role and usefulness. In this moment of stripping away, of death to a former style of life, the Church's ministry must not be to substitute ersatz identities, thus prolonging the irreligious game, but to celebrate this emptying. The Church can assure the individual that this loss of social identity does not mean death in the religious sense.[5]

What do these understandings of how adults develop say to the church? First, they suggest that we need to take seriously the dynamics going on in people's lives in the natural progression of the adult life cycle in program planning. It is important for people of similar ages, dealing with much the same life concerns, to be able to share them with others in the context of their church.

For example, one large congregation structures its Sunday morning educational program around the decades of life with "tracks" of topics of particular interest to each age group—each track primarily for those in their 20s, 30s, 40s, 50s, or 60s plus.

A younger age group may be discussing faith issues and children, and an older group may be focusing on the impact of retirement on spirituality. The possibilities are reflective of the expressed needs of the people at each age period.

An apparent drawback is the tendency to generalize needs by age groups. This problem is handled by making it clear that *anyone* can be part of *any* group, so if grandma wants to dialogue with young adults about faith and the singles' scene, more power to her. Older parents, without young children, often participate with the parenting age groups since they are now *grandparents*. The structure is not rigid, but does clearly utilize an understanding of the adult life cycle in structuring the church's educational program. Conversely, there is also a place for intergenerational activities, where people of various ages can share with each other. Again, our understanding of the adult life cycle can give direction to our planning.

The findings of the FD/ALC study also suggest that the church, in its many forms, needs to more fully celebrate the transitions of adulthood ritually, as it does those of childhood and youth. Rites such as baptism, bar mitzvah, confirmation, marriage, and the funeral celebrate the early years and the end of life, but there are very few, if any, significant ritualistic celebrations for most adults during the half-century or more span from marriage to death, other than as parents in those focusing on children and youth. What about a new job? Retirement? Becoming a grandparent? These are times of life transition. Are they not also times for that mixture of celebration and reflection that symbolizes meaningful ritual in the faith community?

As individuals, we can better understand ourselves through greater awareness of some of the predictable patterns of adult development. At a workshop for those in midlife, a young man of 29 said—part humorously, but very seriously—that he wanted to learn what the "mid-life crisis" is all about before it hit him. That's planning ahead!

This understanding of adulthood provides a context for our faithing experiences, and the integration of faith development as a central and vital element of one's total life development. As has been noted earlier in the chapter, the faithing process continues—in one form or another—throughout life. The degree to which it is integrated into the totality of the adult life cycle can provide fuller meaning for each of us throughout our adult years.

Before ending this chapter, I want to add one postscript. Predictably, most of the focus of the FD/ALC study was on the *faith development* side of the equation. However, there is an important dimension of faith in our attitudes toward the *adult life cycle* aspect also. Some of life's basic questions come to mind: What does it mean to be a human being? What does it mean to be born? To really live? To procreate? To age? To die? What is the meaning of "adult" for the aged person in her or his final years, dependent—like a child—on others for food and care? How really little significant theological reflection there is on these themes. It is a void that needs to be reclaimed.

For Reflection

1. If, as the FD/ALC study suggests, people are aware of a "midlife crisis" in their lives, why do they not see its relationship to their faith development as clearly? Is it because people's faith is so firm that it is not affected by midlife change? Or, is it that people do not perceive much, if any, significant relationship between their faith and other life transitions? Or are there still other reasons? What does this say to us as individuals? What does it say to us as religious leaders?
2. In what ways do theories of *adult* development—like those of Havighurst, Erikson, Levinson, Sheehy, and others—help us in our understanding of our *faith* development?
3. Reflect on the unusual use of "uselessness" as a spiritual concept for the retirement years, and the Whitehead quotation used in the chapter. What are your reactions? Positive? Negative? Why?
4. From the perspective of *your* personal faith, what would you have said to the woman who asked "How can you joke about growing older?" Is there a relationship between humor and faith?

CHAPTER SIX

FAITH AND CRISIS

Life Changes and Faith Development

BEFORE WE BEGIN, IT MAY BE WISE TO CONSIDER the meaning of the word *crisis*. Unfortunately, we most often use it in reference to a tragedy or extreme anxiety. Usually, it carried a negative connotation. If I am experiencing a crisis in my life, that's *not good*.

In actuality, a crisis can be either positive or negative. What is important is that it denotes *radical change*. A dictionary definition of the word puts it simply:

> A crucial situation; turning point (from the Greek *krisis*, turning point).

Erikson defines the term similarly, but more broadly:

> ...not a threat of catastrophe, but a turning point, a crucial period of increased vulnerability and heightened potential....[1]

A crisis, therefore, can be a variety of things:...having a baby ...experiencing the death of a loved one...getting fired from a job... being asked to take on new responsibility...getting married...getting divorced...feeling God's presence in answered prayer...dealing with those times that God says "No"....

As we look together at the meaning of *crisis*, we want to expand our perspectives to recognize the positive, as well as the negative overtones of the word. In so doing, the emphasis is on *all* experiences of significant change—positive and negative—in a person's life. Increasingly, writers in the field use terms such as "passages," "transitions," and "transformations" as the focal points of their developmental theories. I believe this is good, since these words better help us understand the concept of "turning point" which is so central to any definition of "crisis."

In Chapter Five, we looked at several developmental theories. Havighurst's "developmental tasks" suggest the ongoing necessity of dealing with new challenges throughout life; Erikson's "psychosocial crises" pose alternatives in our responses to life experiences; Levinson emphasizes that times of "transition" alternate with more stable periods in the life journey; and Sheehy's title, *Passages* reaffirms the theme. *Crisis, transition,* and *change* provide the bases for our understanding of human development, particularly adult development.

In a College Board study of participants in adult learning situations, *Americans In Transition,* 83% of the respondents indicated that they were taking an adult education course because of clearly defined *changes* in their life structures.[2] Change, transition...yes, *crisis* experiences are ever with us, and—what is more important—it is as we cope with these experiences that we truly grow. In our increasingly urbanized, computerized, and depersonalized culture, crises often become pivotal catalysts for significant rethinking of values, meanings...and also faith. The College Board study focused on secular adult education, but its findings are also significant for adult faith development. If five out of six men and women take adult education courses because of life transitions, does it not hold logically that a significant majority of people will look to their synagogue, congregation, or parish when they are dealing with life's *spiritual* transitions? Marriage and death come to mind immediately, but what about those in between? If I'm laid off at work, how can my parish give me support? If my son or daughter is on drugs, how can my church help me? If I receive an honor or complete an academic degree, are these not *positive* crises in which my faith community should properly share?

In the previous chapter, we noted that chronological age is not, per se, the most significant factor related to faith development. What did come through, however, is that changes, growth, and new development in one's faith structures *do* appear to occur more during periods of transition or crisis than during times of relative stability. Probably the most strongly affirmed hypothesis in our FD/ALC study was the one that stated:

> There is a relationship between periods of transition, change, and crisis in one's life and one's *faith development.*

It *is* apparent that, for most of us, faith development is more likely to occur during those periods when one's life is in some degree of disequilibrium. The result may be a "stronger" faith, a "weaker" faith, or perhaps just a "different" faith, but the individual's perspective is changed because of ferment at some of life's turning points.

Module 1 was able to establish a correlation between major life events and changes in faith. Module 2 adds an important dimension in noting that those interviewed see faith growth more as a process of "maturing" or "evolving" in response to the challenges of these life experiences. Put another way, it is not so much the *fact* that one has experienced a crisis or transition that affects a person's faith. Rather, it is the way the individual *deals with, learns from,* and *grows spiritually because of* the experience. We can illustrate this by sharing brief biographical stories of two of the people we interviewed in depth for Module 2. These are real people. The names, however, are pseudonyms.

"Marie" is a widow in her late 60s who had recently experienced the loss of loved ones, including the deaths of a son and a sister in an auto accident and, even more recently, the death of her husband. As a child, and in her earlier adult years, she questioned little about her faith. She prayed regularly, trusted God to provide for her needs, and saw life as positive and hopeful. Now, after the deaths and other sorrows, her faith is less trusting and secure. She is actively questioning, even though her minister has urged her not to do so. She describes her faith:

> I don't feel that it's as strong. I pray that I can regain some of the faith I did have, but it's really hard to be alone...maybe everything is just colored a little darker. But I do know I believe in God.... All we have to do is believe.... All we have to do is have faith....[3]

"Marie" holds to her relatively simple faith and has *not* been encouraged by pastor, family, or friends to work through her grieving and her negative feelings. She feels lost and very much alone spiritually. Sadly, the interview suggests that she has not been able to grow much spiritually as a result of her crises.

"Nan," age 41, has experienced other crises and has dealt with them in a different way. Following an unhappy marriage and divorce, she explored a lesbian lifestyle for a time, which was also unfulfilling. As a Jew, she was raised in a Kosher family, but indicates that she only began to develop a relationship with God in college, when new and broader concepts of faith and religion were opened up to her. In the eyes of some, she has "lost her faith," but she perceives it differently. She is now part of a group with whom she celebrates Jewish holidays, and avails herself of other spiritual growth experiences that have, according to her, expanded her faith. She has been able to deal positively with her faith questions and is happier and more fulfilled spiritually because of it.[4]

These are but two examples, but they symbolize many. Crisis and transition come to all of us. The development of a meaningful faith does not just happen because we *have* a crisis; it comes into being as a result of two other factors: the ways in which *others* provide support and encouragement to us at the time of crisis or transition, and the ways *we* are able to deal with it internally.

An intriguing new understanding came out of the study. We heard the words "weaker" and "stronger," "more" or "less" used a good bit by people describing their faith:

> "My faith is *stronger* because of...."
> "Since that experience, I don't have *as much* faith as I used to...."
> "After it happened, my faith became *weaker*..."
> "I have *more* faith now than I did as a teenager...."

Those interviewed—like most everyone else—usually use these or similar comparative terms to describe their faith. We had a difficult time, however, really getting at what was meant by "stronger" or "weaker," "more faith" or "less faith," and the like. The terms are really ambiguous, at least as they refer to faith. As we explored with respondents what they meant, we began to discover an interesting context of meaning on the part of many. A person who is experiencing crisis may well feel that he or she is "losing my faith" (remember

Susan in Chapter Two?) when, in fact, the individual is *actually growing* or *maturing* in her or his faith understanding. However, because this person is exploring *new* faith possibilities, there is a corollary sense of guilt because, at the same time, he or she may well be rejecting and rethinking some of the faith structures that have been a part of her or his whole being since childhood. "Nan" had to deal with the fact that her new understandings of faith put her in conflict with her parents and the traditional Judaism in which she had been raised. It is a paradox of our religious enculturation that a faith that is maturing and developing is often perceived and even described by the individual and others, as *diminishing* because it involves the rethinking *and perhaps rejection* of traditional ideas.

Recently, I was guest leader of the Sunday morning adult forum in a large, suburban Protestant church. As we were discussing topic, a man made the statement:

> We raise our kids in the church and teach them what's right, then they take off to college and *lose their faith*...at a so-called Christian college too!

His words and interpretation illustrate the point that came clear in the FD/ALC study interviews. It may well be that the "kids" are actually maturing in their spiritual development, but since such growth involves new ideas and faith interpretations, it is unfortunately perceived by others—often parents and friends—as being a *loss* of faith.

For individuals, these findings help us better understand that it may well be at those times when life is in turmoil that we truly can find new meaning in our faith. Perhaps it is the "still, small voice of calm" that speaks to us "through earthquake, wind, and fire...," to paraphrase the old hymn, that sees us through life's difficult passages.

In many ways it is through our faithing that a fuller understanding of God's greatness and wonder becomes real. Henry Norris Russell, the astronomer, was lecturing on the Milky Way. A woman in the group asked him, "If the world is so little, and the universe so great, can we really believe that God pays much attention to us?" Russell paused, then said, "That, madam, depends entirely on how big a God you can believe in."

A small book, published a generation ago, proclaimed in its title, *Your God Is Too Small*. How true this is for most of us. It is as we learn from and deal with life's testy transitions that our understanding of God and our faith can mature and develop to their fullest dimensions.

For those in ministry, the implications of the research seem clear. We who minister effectively must be particularly sensitive to the needs of our people during their periods of change and transition. The church, the parish, and the synagogue have traditionally celebrated life's transitions *ceremonially* through baptism, bar or bat mitzvah, marriage, and the memorial of the funeral. These are the public celebrations of life that are the central core of the church's ministry. At these times, clergy usually are personally involved in a one-to-one basis: the pastor prays with the bereaved, the rabbi prepares the young person for the bar or bat mitzvah ceremony, the priest counsels the engaged couple. All this is good and vital and important.

But I believe there is another form of *crisis ministry* that most churches have *not* explored or developed as fully. This involves bringing together people experiencing the same or similar transition experiences. Alcoholics Anonymous is successful because every participant at its meetings is an alcoholic, and admits it. They find strength to deal with their problems together.

As a pastor many years ago, I was in a marital counseling relationship with three couples at the same time. Although the problems of each were different, there were enough commonalities that I asked each couple if they would be willing to be a part of a small group, with the other two couples, to work together on their problems. "Who are the others?" was the response from each, but that remained my secret until the appointed evening when the seven of us met in a comfortable but private room at the church. At first, the sharing was guarded, but after several times together, they developed an openness and concern for each other that not only helped each couple deal with *its* own problems, but established a strong and deep bond of friendship and support for one another. They *ministered to each other* in ways I could never do. The church had gone an extra step to try to help people in crisis.

Perhaps an even better illustration of ministry to those sharing a common crisis occurred in 1986, about a week after the tragic explosion of the space shuttle Challenger. People of every nation, every creed, every style of life were united in their mourning. Churches, synagogues, faith communities of all kinds held services of memorial for the victims.

About a month later, at a conference of religious leaders, a woman shared this moving experience that had taken place in her Catholic parish:

> We are still in shock from the Challenger tragedy, but I want to share how our parish helped its members. We had remembered the astronauts who lost their lives during Mass the following Sunday morning—we had dealt with it ceremonially.
>
> Then our priest made a simple statement from the pulpit: "If any of you would like to meet with me in the fellowship hall after Mass just to talk about this, you're welcome to come."
>
> He had no idea how many people would respond...perhaps a dozen or so? Actually, more than 100 people gathered in that room that morning. Our pastor suggested we just talk together in small groups about our feelings. "Be honest," he said, "if you want to curse God about this, go ahead and do so, but express yourselves in any way you want to."
>
> Forty-five minutes later, the priest called us all together for a moment of prayer, then he had to leave for the next Mass. One by one the small groups disbanded, but some remained well into the second hour.

What a beautiful illustration of how faith can be reborn and nurtured, can mature and become real in times of crisis. Here is an example of a pastor and parish who were sensitive that people were hurting. The service of memorial was meaningful, but it was only as they went a step *beyond the ceremonial function* and became intimately involved together in their common grief that the healing of faith could really begin.

What was played out in worldwide grief can also happen for individuals and in the faith community. A young mother finds that she has cancer and her years may be numbered. Her emotional and spiritual equilibrium are upset; she searches for meaning from the mystery of life; she struggles to pray and often grapples with her most basic questions and doubts. She feels alone. She may share her feelings with family and friends, perhaps even with pastor, priest, or rabbi, but how can the *faith community as a whole* minister to this woman? Is there not a place for support groups and other ways by which *several* persons sharing a common experience *can help each other grow in their faith* as they deal with crisis in their lives? When bad things happen to good people, one often needs more than the traditional adult education class to fully cope.

As I visit churches, parishes, and synagogues, more and more often I am seeing, listed on the weekly bulletin, simple announcements indicating that the church's ministry *is* there at points of common needs:

AIDS Support Group: Tuesday, 8:00 P.M.
FPCD (Fellowship of Parents of Children on Drugs): Friday at 7
Midlife Men in Vocational Change: Sundays after the Service

And so they go. This is the church in ministry to those in *crisis*!

What about those facing retirement and fearful of it? What about the woman who has raised her family and is entering the work force, possibly for the first time, at age 40? What about the couple with their first newborn—the greatest life transition of all. They've read the books and talked with the pediatrician. They feel fairly secure in handling the baby's physical needs, but there is a deeper hunger. What does it mean to be a parent, to create with God a new human life? What can we do to help this child grow as fully as possible "in wisdom and in stature, and in favor with God and man" (Luke 2:52 RSV)?

There is no single answer. For some, a ministry to those in crisis may come through small discussion groups. For others, it could involve helping them find appropriate reading material. For still others, a prayer circle may minister most fully. Whatever it be, it is at the points of change, transition, or crisis that people *most need* the spiritual nurture of their parish, congregation, or synagogue. Those communities of faith that are sensitive to and provide ministries for these people are living out their greatest commission to the fullest.

If anything came clear in the study, it is that people in transition are particularly ready, emotionally and spiritually, for faith development. Our program of ministry must start where the people are and build its ministry on their needs. Too long have our programs of adult education been based on what we—the church—want our people to learn. Perhaps it is time to turn everything around and start at the point of the needs and problems, transitions and crises of our people. That is where *they* are. That is where the church should be also.

For Reflection

1. Reflect on one or more crisis experiences in your life, either positive or negative, that had an impact on your faith. What happened and how did you respond...at first? Later? What factors (people? reading? a group? personal prayer? other?) were most helpful to you in the process?

2. If negative life experiences tend to lead to a sense of decreased faith, how can the church help its people deal with those crises and utilize them toward *positive* spiritual growth? ("When life gives you lemons...make lemonade!")

3. This chapter notes the intriguing paradox that people who are actually growing in their faith may well report that they have "less faith" now than previously because of those elements of previous faith stances they have had to give up. How have you seen this happen in your life? In the lives of others?

4. The story of one parish's response to the Challenger tragedy is a graphic example of a ministry responding to an entire group's needs. Think of situations you may know where the church was able to minister to a whole people in crisis.

CHAPTER SEVEN

"SPIRITUAL" OR "RELIGIOUS"?

Individual Faith Development and the Church

A TALK-SHOW HOST WAS INTERVIEWING AN ACTOR who had just completed a blockbuster biblical epic. He posed the question directly: "Are you *religious*?" There was a moment of silence, and the camera showed that the actor was choosing his words carefully before answering. "Let's just say I'm *'spiritual.'*" The host tried to probe his meaning further, but the actor was loathe to say more, so they turned to another topic.

"Spiritual" or "religious"? We found similar responses from more than two-thirds of those interviewed in the FD/ALC study. We wondered, at first, if this was just some "antics with semantics," but as the pattern appeared again and again, we began to probe for what people perceived to be the meanings of the words.

"Religious" is seen by many people to refer to the rituals and dogmas, structures and programs of the institutional church. Generally, "religious" persons are perceived as those actively identified with a synagogue, parish, or local church. They serve on boards and committees, are usually present not only for regular services but also for most special events. Being "religious" does not *necessarily* need to indicate that one has a deep faith or an active prayer life. Its connotation is primarily one of *involvement*. "She's very religious" usually means "she's a good church worker."

"Spiritual" is used as the metaphor for the personalization of religion. "Spiritual" persons may or may not be active in any faith community, but are those for whom faith is continually nurtured through prayer, meditation, challenging books, honest talks with friends, simple beauties of nature, art and music and the like. The "spiritual" person may well find this nurture in the context of the faith community, but may just as likely find it outside the church.

Two of our interviewees put it succinctly. "Kathy," a Catholic, was refused absolution by her priest at confession because she was using birth control pills prescribed by her doctor for a health problem. This led to disenchantment with the church and a changing perspective on her faith.

> If I really want to communicate with my God, it's through people and through nature and not through church...no, I don't find it there. Definitely through people.[1]

If asked, "Kathy" would undoubtedly feel more comfortable with the word "spiritual" than "religious" for herself.

"Doug," a black school superintendent in his fifties, attends a Baptist church where he feels supported and understood. He is very specific about the two terms. He differentiates between being "religious" as "performing the rituals of the church" and "spiritual" as having a spiritual outlook and an intimate connection to God through daily "communication." Yet, he has a deep love and concern for the church.

> We have to somehow overcome the grip religion has so that the only place of worship must not be the church and that rather than spend such a great deal of time on maintenance and upkeep of the church building, we're going to have to concentrate on whatever it is that ties for me my inner peace and whatever it is that ties for you your inner peace....[2]

These persons and many others who were interviewed reflected essentially similar meanings for the terms. On the surface, the differentiation may appear simple. At a deeper level, however, these definitions reflect a very real theological tension between concepts of *individuality* and *community* in matters of faith. It is not difficult for the individual to profess that faith can best be expressed personally, and to suggest (at least by implication) that the worship and activities of the church can actually be hindrances to this spiritual development. One layman stated it simply: "I believe in Christianity, not 'churchianity.'" In our study, there were numerous reports that religious institutions or religious training had been a significant factor in shaping *negative* attitudes toward religion. In the Module 1 Gallup survey, when asked where they would turn when faced with a problem or crisis, of a list of nine choices, "seek help from a religious counselor" was ranked *sixth*, and "discuss it with a class or group at your church or synagogue" was ranked *last*. (See the data chart on page 40 that substantiates this.) It is apparent, at least from these findings, that relatively few respondents saw the traditional structures and formats of the faith community as major resources at times of difficulty or personal crisis.

There are some who are critical of the theory and concept of faith development precisely around this issue, arguing that it places too much emphasis on *individual faith* and too little on the importance of interpersonal relationships in the faith exploration. This criticism has merit and should not be taken lightly. However, most of those critical of the church do not necessarily have problems with "interpersonal relationships" per se. Rather, they feel that most churches overemphasize ritual and inflexible tradition to a degree that faithing through interpersonal relationships becomes extremely difficult.

Some have equated this attitude toward the church as roughly equivalent to an adult's feelings about his or her parents. In most cases, parents are respected and loved, yet the very process of establishing one's own identity as fully adult necessitates some reaction to the parental lifestyle in which we were raised.

Sometimes it may even involve the rejection of values held dear by our parents. Similarly, with the church relationship, if I am to mature in my own faith, I may have to react to elements of my faith upbringing and seek for myself a faith identity that is wholly mine. Perhaps this is but one other example of human nature in which we are often more critical of those persons and institutions for which we have the greatest affection. If so, then perhaps the strongly voiced critique of the church may actually be seen as a *form of affirmation.*

We must, however, give equal time to the other side of this discussion. We must never forget that the faith community, for all its faults and weaknesses, *is* the organizational force that has sustained peoples' faith, in its various expressions, for centuries. A speaker at one of our conferences reviewing the FD/ALC study said it sensitively and well:

> Religion...has the corrective in that...(it)...continues to span culture and helps us see from the perspective of community in ways that our individualistic cultural spectacles often lose sight of.

Valid concern has been expressed about some negative images of the institutional church that were reflected in the study's findings. "We know it's there, and may agree with it, but we don't like it!" one speaker stated forcefully. Others spoke of their own internal love/hate relationship with formalized religion. Recognizing the importance of *individual* faith development, many persons, myself included, express the concern that the individualistic approach, in itself, is not enough, and "the theology of faith *community* needs to be restructured." That is a central purpose of this book.

Module 1 of the FD/ALC study, the Gallup survey, reports a high correlation between faith change and participation in organized religion. It indicates that the majority of people active in the church give significantly more thought to living a worthwhile life, their relation to God, the value of life, and the developing of faith than those not so involved.

	Percentage indicating importance of...			
	Living a worthwhile life	Relationship with God	Meaning and value of life	Developing one's faith
All respondents	67%	59%	58%	47%
Church or synagogue members	73%	71%	62%	60%
—More active now than at age 16	78%	78%	68%	70%
—No change	73%	65%	52%	51%
—Less active now than at age 16	65%	63%	59%	48%
Non-member of church or synagogue	57%	44%	52%	31%

Module 2 finds a similar positive correlation. However, since it involved face-to-face dialogue interviews, and therefore was able to probe more deeply into meanings, Module 2 also indicates that involvement in the religious community, per se, is not as much a factor in one's faith development as is the *quality* of that experience. Those who report church relationships that sponsor or encourage the spiritual quest and the exploration of meaning find that it is this *active searching process* in the context of the faith community, not membership or routine participation alone, that makes the difference.

What do I mean by "sponsoring or encouraging the spiritual quest"? Quite simply, it means that the synagogue, parish, or congregation is doing more than carrying out familiar and traditional rituals and procedures. There is a sense of vibrancy in the program and intensity of *concern about people*. Decisions are made not only on the basis of "what is our denomination's policy" or "we never did it that way before" (sometimes referred to as the "Seven Last Words of the Church"), but even more in terms of "what are our people's needs today?" and "which approach will best help men and women grow in their personal faith?"

Let's explore some specific meanings for ministry.

More Use of Small Face-to-Face Groups

A recurring criticism of the church is that it does not provide enough opportunity for people to talk *together* about their faith questions and concerns. Although the "small group movement" has been highly visible in educational circles for decades and many churches *do* have adult classes and small groups, the fact still remains—based on the FD/ALC study and countless workshops and conferences on the subject—that most religious adult education still follows the traditional lecture format, with a high value being placed on *how many* persons are in attendance—*the more, the better*. Interaction is primarily in the form of questions to the speaker and the exchange of ideas among the participants is relatively seldom an integral and important part of the learning experience.

There are notable exceptions, however. Several years ago, I was asked to preach at a Catholic parish in another state. When the priest of that parish invited me, by telephone, he indicated but one condition: "You'll have to do it our way!" This phrase conjured up a whole passel of images as to what he meant, until he clarified it quite simply.

The experience, for me, was one of the most fulfilling preaching relationships I have ever had.

Although there were hundreds of people at each of the parish's two Masses, the homily time involved *people interaction*. I was given only 5-6 minutes to speak, to present one or two points for the people to consider. Then small groups of 4-6 people formed themselves, some turning around to talk to those in the pew behind them, to discuss what I had said. After about five minutes, the presiding priest asked them to turn their attention again to the front and asked for reflections. Members of several small groups stood randomly to share a thought or two that had come up in their conversation. I then had one minute for summary and closure.

What an experience! Rather than being a one-way street, the sermon had input, reflection and dialogue, and sharing. Everyone in that church was participating. That's real face-to-face involvement!

I do not propose that all sermons or homilies must necessarily involve buzz groups. In that parish, it was a part of their ongoing experience and had meaning for them; the degree that this model would work elsewhere would depend on many factors. What is important in this illustration, however, is that we in the church must more fully explore ways in which we can better enable our people to *talk together* about their faith.

George Gallup, Jr., President of the Gallup Organization, in *Faith Development and Your Ministry*, his book based on the FD/ALC study, urges "...churches and synagogues...to 'think small'—to encourage the formation of small prayer fellowship or Bible study groups."[3] Gallup quotes Jim McManus in the *National Catholic Reporter* writing about "lay communities, or small Catholic groups," which represent "an important trend within the U.S. church.... They take religion, and the need for religious community, seriously."[4]

He quotes Rabbi Harold Schulweis, of Encino, California, who decries what he calls "the impersonalization of the synagogue..." and suggests:

> How can we talk peoplehood when people haven't experienced people?...The synagogue must be...divided into groups of families, into clusters of congregational families who pledge to celebrate Jewish life, to learn together, to grow Jewishly together.[5]

Gallup also echoes the words of Presbyterian William Russell:

> The rediscovery of the small group as a method of nurturing and multiplying believers offers the local congregation the opportunity for spiritual and numerical growth that many churches are seeking today. Not since the introduction of the Sunday school in England by Robert Raikes has there been a more exciting possibility for growth and change among New Testament churches.[6]

Catholic, Jewish, Protestant...all affirming the importance of the small group in today's ministry. So what else is new? Small groups have been touted and tried for decades and, many would say, haven't worked. I challenge that! The reason small, face-to-face groups have had difficulty is 1) we tend to judge success by large numbers, 2) small groups are hard to administer, and 3) *we have not really encouraged our people to speak openly together in the religious setting.*

It's much easier to hire an "expert" to lecture to a relatively large group of adults than to plan and organize a dozen small groups so that people can talk together in a more intimate way. We have *taught* rather than enabling men and women to *share and learn together.* In a local church retreat I led several years ago, the group began to deal with some real life issues, but one woman was visibly uncomfortable. "Do you really expect me to talk about such *personal* things with *church people?*" she asked. There was a long silence. Finally, a man responded: "If you can't share them with your church friends, who can you share them with?" One reason small face-to-face groups do not always work is that we leaders of the faith community have not helped our people learn to talk...with others...about our faith...in church.

Small groups do not necessarily need to be formally structured within the church's adult education program. They can take a variety of forms and meet in all sorts of places, for example:

●the six midlife women who run their own small businesses and meet weekly for lunch to talk about what it means to be a woman and (for them) Christians in today's business world;

●the "Twigbenders"—three couples, each with pre-school children, who meet twice monthly with their parish worker to discuss some of the ticklish faith questions their children ask (or may ask);

•the seven men who meet Tuesday mornings at 6:00 A.M. in a local coffee shop for Bible study and prayer before going to work;

•the eight Jewish men and women who meet monthly with their Rabbi to reflect and pray together about how they can keep their Jewish faith vital in a culture in which they are a minority;

•the "lunch bunch," a dozen men and women who work in the same factory and who, sitting on packing boxes, have sack-lunch discussions with their pastor Wednesdays at noon;

•the five neighborhood mothers from three different churches and a synagogue who meet twice a week for morning coffee in one of their kitchens. As they put it, "Tuesday is serious—scripture study and prayer; Thursday is woman talk, but still a lot of real meaningful conversation"; and finally,

•the three couples in a Florida church, mentioned in Chapter Six, who first came together to talk about their marital problems with their pastor. Several years later, their marriages more secure, they still meet regularly because, as one of them puts it, "That's where we really grow in our faith."

The small, face-to-face group is a vitally important way of "sponsoring and encouraging the spiritual quest." Elie Wiesel put it simply:

> Let two human beings become one and the world is no longer the same; let two human creatures accept one another and creation will have meaning....[7]

Pastoral Care

The taped interviews and transcripts in Module 2 are powerful reminders of how pain and agony are a natural part of life. Many times in the interview process people began to weep during poignant moments in their life histories, indicating how many small and large burdens people carry with them from day to day and sometimes over several decades.

Both Module 1 and Module 2 samples indicate that people are as likely to work through a crisis on their own as to share it with close friends. Most of them (60%) would likely *not* seek help from a religious counselor. It may be, as some have suggested, that they will turn to family or friends first before going to the clergyperson or other religious professional. Peer support is important for people. However, the findings from Module 2 point out that many adults who need the help of a trained and effective pastoral counselor often hesitate because they fear they will be "judged" for their "lack of faith."

There is evidence from the FD/ALC study that many adults are dealing with strong unresolved tensions that they may well not recognize. They may not be willing or able to go to a psychiatrist, but a skilled and sensitive pastoral or spiritual counselor can often help them open up painful memories and find ways to help them heal themselves in the context of a supportive faith.

Another significant finding in the FD/ALC study is the problem, faced by an unusual number of adults, of coming to terms with one's changing relationship with parents. Many of those interviewed told stories of having a strong sense of their own identity until they were with their parents, at which time they became, figuratively, children again. One woman put it: "I'm an adult and act like one except when I am with my mother—then I become a little girl both to her and to myself." For many, this was a major problem. Establishing one's spirituality, individuality, and personal faith *apart from* parental models and expectations seems to be a key task for psychosocial and faith growth.

A religious leader can demonstrate her or his sensitivity to faith issues and stages by the language and examples used in preaching and teaching. Knowing that a range of faith stages and needs will cut across the membership of any congregation, the pastor can be intentional about selecting metaphors and life experiences that speak to such a range. One pastor who preaches regularly put it simply, using Fowler's structure of faith stages:

> Although I may not know who is who, I have to assume that
> there is a mixture of Faith Stage 2s, 3s, 4s, 5s, and maybe even
> some 6s attending worship on Sunday morning. As I preach, I
> try, by illustration or insight, to touch each of them, wherever
> they are on their faith journey, somewhere in the sermon.
> Stage theory helps me understand and speak to the individual
> differences, and yet the wholeness of my congregation.[8]

Changing the Norms in Faith Communities

It became evident from the study and from comments made at many conferences and workshops on the topic that, unfortunately, the faith community that encourages the nurturing of faith journeys among its members *is far too rare.* Jean Haldane found that the marks of "relig-ious socialization" in one Protestant parish were: 1) to belong, 2) to be active, 3) to adopt the appropriate language, 4) to support the growth of the parish, and 5) *to keep quiet about religious differences.*[9] Because of these *implicit* norms, members were *discouraged* from sharing their faith or spiritual experiences, their struggles, doubts, or joys. This kind of resistance to the sharing of personal faith actually functions to block a rich resource for faithing, and it certainly is not limited to the one parish Haldane surveyed—*it applies to churches in nearly all religious traditions.*

Religious communities need to engage their members in conversa-tions about how they experience their faith. Instead of being told what to believe, people need to be helped to identify, for themselves, what spiritual resources they can and do call upon to make decisions, face crises, and explore their questions and doubts. They need to be helped to reflect upon all aspects of their lives as "faithing experiences."

It may be that the institutional church resists this kind of explora-tion for fear that individuals may diverge too much from the tradi-tional norms when given the chance to personalize their faith. Howev-er, the opposite is just as likely to happen if the opportunity is provided with intentionality and integrity. When people are enabled to see their faith journeys *as parallels to* the ways in which God has faithfully worked with others throughout the ages, they are helped to connect their personal experiences with the traditions of their own faith community.

Group norms are slow to change, but the freeing of people to ex-plore for themselves their own faith stories and those of others about them strengthens not only the individuals but the life of the corporate community as well.

Ministry to the Unchurched

The significant Gallup study on "The Unchurched American" found that the unchurched in America are, more often than not, persons with religious convictions and a personal faith. They just happen not to participate in the life of the church or synagogue.[10] Other studies have corroborated this position, and it was clearly underlined through the in-depth interviews of Module 2. The unchurched respondents to both the Module 1 and Module 2 surveys, for the most part, indicated that they believe in God, read the Bible and other religious books, pray, and reflect upon life's meaning. They consider themselves "spiritual" but not "religious."

Why, then, do they *not* attend worship services or become involved in a religious community? The findings suggest that a particular event (or series of events) in one's past connected with a church or religious leader often turned the relationship "sour" and the person simply left the fellowship. Many reported that nobody even called on them to ask why.

Studies, including ours, also indicate that the unchurched tend to be more accepting of changing personal values and ethics than are many church members. Churches that are concerned about a ministry to those outside their membership will take seriously a thorough self-examination of potential stumbling blocks for the unchurched. Some obstacles may be codes of conduct, judgments of unacceptable lifestyles or, as one of our subjects puts it, "a sour pickle religion where everything is condemnation."

Many voices have expressed feelings that educational or social programs are usually planned only for the *membership* of the congregation, synagogue, or parish, with little effort being made to provide strong invitations to the larger community. One woman pastor, however, indicated that she promotes her church's adult education courses openly through the local newspaper, radio, and even posters in stores with a strong message that *anyone interested* is welcome. Church members echo this spirit with word-of-mouth invitations and the word is out that they really mean it! She indicates that this strategy involves an average of about 100 new people a year from *outside* their church's regular participants—about a quarter of whom ultimately become active in the church.

The underlying issue in reaching out to the unchurched appears to be how to communicate that the religious community is *open* to people who question, who are different, who are struggling with the rest of us in making meaning in their lives.

Again, I am aware that this chapter has been hard on the established church. We all know of many local synagogues, parishes, and congregations that *are* truly ministering with *meaning* for their people. We praise them and affirm them as fully as possible.

Unfortunately, however, the research and commentary at dozens of workshops and conferences do indicate a far greater number that are not. It was the hope of those who supported the FD/ALC study that from it might come new insights and understandings to help individuals in their faithing, and clergy and lay leaders in the ways they minister with adults. The FD/ALC Report addresses this concern in detail, while this book can but lift up some of the major themes in a context of reflection and discussion.

"Spiritual" or "religious"? Let us work and let us pray (perhaps at the same time—it's efficient!) that *both* words may find new and vibrant meaning in our faithing. May we who call ourselves "spiritual" find new vitality in a faith that is expressed through the caring and sharing of people in true community. May we who are "religious" be touched also by the spirit of the Living God becoming a vital and growing part of our inner being and manifesting itself through our outer being as people of the spirit.

For Reflection

1. Think about the definitions of "spiritual" and "religious" suggested in this chapter. Do you agree that they reflect the thinking of most people? If not, how would you define the words? What do these perceptions of "spiritual" and "religious" suggest for individual faith development? For the faith community?
2. Think about, and perhaps share with others, small faithing groups of which you are or have been a part, or with which you are familiar in other ways. What makes them special as avenues of faith development?
3. What are some of the "norms" in your faith community? In what ways do they *strengthen* or *hinder* your faith growth? Where they hinder, how can they be changed?
4. Why do church people so often have difficulty reaching outside their own membership to invite and welcome the unchurched? How can we realize and tap the potential of people "on the fringe"?

CHAPTER EIGHT

TOWARD AN ATTITUDE OF LIFELONG FAITHING

Some Faith Tasks of Adulthood

IN CHAPTER ONE WE INTRODUCED THE CONCEPT of "faithing" as a way to express the idea of faith as dynamic, not static. We built upon the adult education team, "lifelong learning," to suggest a corollary for spiritual development, "lifelong faithing."

In subsequent chapters, we have explored several facets of *faithing* as an integral part of adult development. As we come to this final chapter, our focus must be one of future orientation. So what? What does this mean to me? And, of more importance, what am I going to do about it? *Lifelong faithing* necessitates each of us taking the responsibility for his or her own faith journey. It means the recognition that an individual's faith is always "in process" of becoming fully whole. Faithing never ends. It is always *dynamic*.

As our attempt to suggest some rather specific "handles" for the process of faithing, please consider fourteen "developmental tasks of faith." Those of us over 30 will have experienced several already, and many may well be working through one or more as you read these words.

In Chapter Five, we noted Robert Havighurst's concept of the "developmental task." Writing in the late 1940s, he defines it as:

> ...a task which arises at or about a certain period in the life of the individual, successful achievement of which leads to...happiness and to success with later tasks, while failure leads to unhappiness in the individual, disapproval by the society, and difficulty with later tasks.[1]

Havighurst suggests 46 *developmental tasks* for the life span, ranging from "learning to walk" in the first year of life to the several adjustments of life's final years. This concept has become a fundamental principle of developmental theory, and is particularly important for educators, for whom developmental tasks lead naturally to their educational counterpart, the *teachable moment*.

Havighurst's developmental tasks, however, only minimally reflect the dimension of *faith* in the life cycle. The *faith tasks* which follow are but suggestions of areas of faith development in the three major periods of the adult life cycle. Others will spring to mind as you read. I urge you to make notes, to yourself and perhaps for sharing with others, as you go along. As you think of other faith tasks, jot them down and reflect upon them.

What is important is not so much the list itself but the affirmation that one's faith is ever growing, changing, maturing as one undertakes the faith tasks of life's journey. *Faith tasks* are building blocks of spiritual completeness—stepping stones toward the fullest dimension of life's meaning.

In the Young Adult Years

For those who marry—establishing together
a spiritual basis for marriage
Some marriages have little, if any, sense of God in the relationship. Others are based on a spiritual partnership that involves the couple in a strong sense of God's presence in the making of their marriage. Most marriages, however, fall somewhere between these polarities. Each

couple, consciously or unconsciously, establishes some kind of spiritual basis for the marriage during the first few months together. How meaningful this is for them depends upon how seriously they take this faith task of...for most of us... young adulthood.

The spiritual basis of any marriage will be reflected in obvious symbols of faith—grace at meals, church attendance, prayer, the religious education of children—but even more in the subtle nuances of relationship: how they handle conflict, their expressions of concern and love for others, and how they discipline their children. The sexual relationship is usually seen as primarily physical, but its spiritual dimension can be very real for those whose sex life is rooted in a deep sense of love as mutual caring and commitment. The sensitivity of marriage partners to this aspect of their sexuality is a most important expression of their faith.

Certainly, for the newly married couple, the establishment of a spiritual basis for their marriage is one of the most important tasks of their early years together.

For those who do not marry—singleness and commitment

Increasingly, singleness plays a more important role in our social structure. Many are single by choice, having a strong commitment to vocation or a desire to live one's own life. Others covet marriage but find it elusive, and for some it never materializes. For still others, singleness comes, often bitterly, after an unhappy marriage; and for a few it comes in the tragic loss of one very much loved.

Whatever the reason, many young adults must confront the questions of singleness. Am I unattractive? Are my standards too high? Am I out of step with the expectations of society? Am I really *not* interested in marriage with its restrictions and demands?

These issues of self-identity manifest themselves strongly in the young adult years when self-image is still very much in formation. In the midst of the frustrations, it is easy to *blame* God that one has no spouse, or feel that God really does not care. The single young adult needs a sense of support in his or her aloneness, but too often there seems to be no one who cares. Clergy often appear too busy for the needs of young adults, especially those who don't attend church regularly, and churches too often have well established family-oriented patterns that seem irrelevant to the needs of single young adults.

A significant faith task of young adulthood is the finding of a personal sense of identity and worth in the context of singleness. The successful handling of this task will have an important bearing on a person's self-image and sense of identity in the context of a growing faith.

Finding the meaning of vocation
In young adulthood, the sense of idealism is high. The vista of a whole life is stretched out and challenges one to do something significant with it. But the uncertainty of *how* to make the greatest contribution is real and frustrating. For some, vocational decisions present few problems, but for most young adults, a variety of roadblocks plague the establishment of a clear sense of vocational direction.

The word "vocation" relates to a sense of being *called*. Traditionally some professions, such as medicine, education, and ministry, have been seen as *callings*, but most of us have difficulty with this sense of call as we read hundreds of "Help Wanted" ads, participate in a dozen interviews, and finally find ourselves essentially an employee number, an infinitesimally small cog in an impersonal mega-corporation.

Finding a *sense of vocation*, a sense of calling, is a difficult faith task for the young adult.

Dealing with the feeling of social powerlessness
Our culture tells the young adult to wait patiently in the wings for the chance to provide social leadership. The decisions of business, industry, church, government, and education seem to be made by those in mid-life and older. The young adult becomes just a number, a statistic, a piece of machinery, and a small one at that!

The young person's growing faith must confront this frustration and find creative ways to combat that sense of powerlessness. Unfortunately, most young adults handle this problem with varying degrees of success, totally *apart* from the context of faith. Yet one's sense of identity is intrinsic to developing faith. Finding a meaningful expression of self is an important faith task of the young adult years.

Discovering a relevance of religious faith for one's life
Young adulthood is a time of questioning, and often doubting, the religious traditions in which the person was raised. Many tend to drift away from the church relationship in the late teens and early twenties. Young adults need to have a strong sense of their ability to guide and direct their own lives. Just as this suggests independence from parental authority, it may also suggest independence from the need for spiritual support. Religion, church, and faith often seem strangely irrele-

vant to young adults. Sermons appear to be geared to needs other than their own. Churches seem populated primarily by people twenty to sixty years their senior. And even the minister is often viewed as a father/mother figure—someone who symbolizes a *dependency,* and is therefore to be avoided. Too often, the young adult's expression of uncertainty in matters of faith is met by the clergy less with understanding and support than with chastisement that one is straying from the tenets of the church.

Yet it is in this context that the patterns of one's *adult faith* are being established. It may well be that the groping for a sense of "the purpose of it all"—the search for life's meaning—is the most important faith task of all for the young adult years.

In the Middle Adult Years

Finding security in a time of midlife changes

In their late 30s and early 40s, both men and women become profoundly aware that their lives are changing much faster than before. He comes to realize that he is not going to be president of the company; she is increasingly reminded that her maturing children need less and less of her motherly ministrations; he reflects more and more on what he is really seeking in life; she may be adjusting to a new identity as a mid-life student, in a new job, or in increased responsibilities outside the home. Such change can be upsetting. It disturbs established patterns. We long for rootage in value systems of the past, yet we seek new expressions for the present. We need anchors of faith that will hold firm in times of change, yet give us the freedom to continue growing.

To meet the challenges of midlife change, men and women must reexamine those things that are most important to them. One's faith also needs reviewing, reaffirming, and perhaps rebuilding. Unfortunately, church tradition has too often viewed questioning and rethinking of faith as negative, and unquestioning and unthinking acceptance of faith issues as positive. Midlife is a time when the rethinking and renewing of one's faith—bringing it into a new focus for the present and setting its tone for the future—should be encouraged and affirmed as an important part of human development.

For those married—re-establishing the marriage relationship
For the typical family, during the twenty to thirty years when children are in the home, husband and wife roles are played primarily in the family context. Decisions are made in the light of family plans; differences are settled according to what is "best for the children"; individual identities, particularly those of the wife/mother, are subordinated to what seems best for the family. *Family* is the larger construct about which its members relate their lives and activities.

But with midlife comes radical change for both parents. One by one, children spin off from the family orbit into lives of their own. Husband and wife are now very different people from who they were when first married. He may be frustrated with his job while she may be excited about reentry into the vocational arena. Individualizing interests point each to new contacts, new friendships, new relationships, and new activities, many of which exclude the spouse. Sex plays a smaller part in their relationship and this reminds them of their other bodily changes. The longing for new experiences may lead to romantic affairs and independent behavior that can further strain the marriage bonds. Is it any wonder that so many marriages fall apart in midlife; and those that stay together usually do so primarily because of the real effort of one or both partners?

The reestablishing of the marriage relationship is a central faith task for most married midlifers. Many of its roots go back to the first faith task of young adulthood. If a spiritual basis did not have high priority in young adulthood, it may emerge as an important marital dynamic in midlife. Each partner must bring both personal needs and those of the spouse into a new mutuality in the context of common values.

For many—adapting to new lifestyles
Death and increasing divorce brings about changes in lifestyle for a growing percentage of midlife adults. The widowed role is different from that of the mother; separation or divorce means long periods of loneliness; a new marriage may bring different religious ideas and traditions (or lack of them) that test one's beliefs. The individual sees possibilities for the faith structure that were not there before. Some are welcome; others are threatening.

The support of one's church is vital. A woman, age 43, who had recently been divorced, put it this way:

For the past twenty-five years, I have been surrounded by

family, but within the last year, my daughter married and
moved to the West Coast, my son went away to college, and
my husband traded me in on a "younger model." All of a sud-
den I'm totally alone. My friends are preoccupied with their
families, and my church doesn't give a damn!

These are strong words from a person who is struggling with a central issue of midlife. Her comments about her church are scathing, but,
unfortunately, too often accurate. Although over one-third of church
members are *not* married, church and synagogue programs usually focus on couples, children, and families, with too little concern for those
who are alone. Even "Family Night Potluck Suppers" suggest that the
single is not fully welcome.

Adapting to new lifestyles may require finding a different understanding of the meaning of one's faith. Those for whom midlife brings
new social relationships may find that search to be their most compel-
ling faith task for this period of their lives.

Dealing with physical aging and the reality of death

In the late 30s we first notice that the old body reacts more slowly
than it did before. In the 40s we discover gray hairs and body aches
that tell us we are slowing down. By the 50s we are critically aware
that, physically, the old gray mare really "ain't what she used to be."
In today's culture, most men and women are dealing *constructively*
with physical aging. Midlifers are more active—jogging, playing ten-
nis, skiing, swimming—than in any previous generation. We take better care of our bodies and probably will live longer because of it. However, we are still quite aware that the aging process is at work, and
although we resist it, we become increasingly sensitive to its end result—old age and death.

The reality of death takes on a new significance. A younger colleague dies of a heart attack, and we wonder about what it is like to
experience death. A loved one dies of cancer before her time, and we
ponder whether we could have faced death with the spirit and trust
she exemplified.

An awareness of the inevitability of death plays an increasing part
in our self-identity as we move into midlife, and with it comes reflection on the meaning of life itself. "What is beyond death's door?" becomes the relevant question in midlife, and with it comes the necessity
of finding answers within one's own theology of life and death. One
examines the beliefs of our church and finds them sustaining, lacking,

or somewhere in between. One discusses the subject with others, but ultimately each person must make *personal* preparation for life's final reality. It is a central faith task of the middle years.

Sharing of self with others

As we have already noted, Erik Erikson suggests that *generativity* is a central need for those in midlife. He defines generativity as the ability to share something of one's self with others, particularly those of a younger generation. This is a critical need of midlife. It is an expression of our faith to want to reflect life's ultimate meanings in ways that speak to the searching of others. To do this, of course, requires that we ourselves have a clear understanding of our faith and values. When we do, our greatest joy is to *share* that understanding.

In the Older Adult Years

Adjusting to retirement and loss of power

Although most people welcome the leisure and lessened responsibility that comes with retirement, these pleasures bring with them a loss of power and the strong sense of the beginning of life's final chapter. Older adults must meet this critical transition with poise and a sense of the ongoing quality of life that passes the torch of responsibility from one generation to another. What makes the transition of retirement particularly difficult for many people is its sense of *finality*. It is not the same as previous vocational change. For many, retirement closes a door to one's active participation in life and begins a terminal chapter that may seem to be more like an epilogue than part of the ongoing story.

For others, however, this image is grossly overdrawn. With increasing longevity and opportunity for travel, activity, and social life, today's senior citizens need not close up the shop of life at 65 or 70. But always lurking beneath the exterior of active golden years is the awareness that one's primary productive life is past.

A person's basic attitude toward aging is central to her or his sense of integrity in later adulthood. Faith grapples with the ultimate issues of life. It is the task of the older adult to find meaning and fulfillment in one's final years.

Keeping mentally and spiritually alert

As one moves into older adulthood, it is easy to become sluggish in body, mind, and spirit. In the later years, these aspects of being need exercise as never before. This is the time to take a swim, to read a book, to enroll in class, to keep growing in faith.

Too many churches assume that their older members are "set in their ways," and miss the golden opportunity to stimulate creative and constructive thinking and discussion around faith issues. Older adults should be encouraged to keep growing spiritually as well as mentally. One 80- "going on 50"-year-old man made the refreshing remark in a discussion group: "I try never to let a day go by without a new idea or thought by which my faith grows." What a marvelous attitude toward faith!

Adjusting to changing cultural values and patterns

The older adult must also find a creative identity within the rapidly changing mainstream of society. For most people over 70, there is more social change now in five years than there was in the first 50 years of their lives. Adjustment does not come easily. One may long for the "good old days" and hope that by ignoring present patterns that past can be brought back, but it will not happen.

Living with change is a faith task because it relates the reality of life (changing) to the anchors of faith (those things we believe are unchanging). This may involve the rethinking of faith structures that have been held for years; but such reflection can open up new understandings and bring revitalized meaning to life. For the older adult, the faith task of coping successfully with the rapid change all around is both challenging and rewarding, and can be the source of life's greatest fulfillment.

Personal preparation for death

Perhaps the ultimate faith task—begun in midlife—is that which relates to the acceptance of one's mortality and the spiritual preparation for death. As the years pass, and one by one friends and loved ones precede us in death, we cannot help pondering the age-old questions:

- •Is there anything beyond?
- •What will it be like?
- •Will I remember this life?
- •Will I be with those I love again?

Religion seeks to provide answers, but ultimately every person must find valid *personal* answers. There is no greater testimony to one's faith than the words: "I'm ready; I'm at peace" spoken by one in life's final days. We who are younger find them difficult to understand because we ourselves are *not* ready—*we still have so many things to do*. What we cannot fully understand is that, in the fullness of time, the person of faith experiences a sense of completion that makes death the natural and easy next step.

Unfortunately, there are some who do not experience such fulfillment and who spend their final years in frustration and despair, from which death is but a blessed release. For others, senility beclouds the mind so that they are unable to express their feelings with clarity. But for those whose faith is alive and whose mind is clear perhaps the final faith task is the most rewarding. "I'm ready; I'm at peace" is the fullest expression of a life well-lived.

For Reflection

1. These *faith tasks* are but suggestions. What other ones come to mind as important? Develop them a bit, in your mind or in conversation with others.

2. What are the strengths and weaknesses of suggesting certain faith tasks for *specific* periods of adulthood, since individuals will probably deal with some faith issues at several different times in their lives? Would it be better to avoid age-designations? Why or why not?

3. In terms of today's society, what are the pluses and minuses of suggesting separate tasks for *married* and *single* persons? To what extent and in what ways are an *individual's* faith tasks related to marriage, divorce, singleness, couples living together (both opposite sex and same sex), or other male/female dynamics?

4. In what ways may the rapidly increasing numbers of those over 65 affect the faith tasks of current and future generations of older adults? Try to visualize what a retirement community may be like in 2020. What new social dynamics may be in force? How will these, and longer lives, affect people's *faithing*?

OPTIONAL GROUP EXPERIENCES

These exercises provide an opportunity for individuals to build upon the content of each chapter in a group experience. They go beyond the "For Reflection" discussion questions at the end of the chapters to provide a fuller involvement with each topic.

There are many variables in groups—age range of members, whether they are close friends or casual acquaintances, formal or informal settings, and others. It is, therefore, impossible to outline *precise* directions for these exercises. The group leader will have to modify and adapt the procedures suggested to fit the specific group situation.

In each case, the exercise is suggested for a period of approximately one hour. Again, adaptation may be necessary. Most of them can easily be amplified to a longer time frame, and in some cases, they could be shortened a bit. In any case, the time available and suggested activities need to be carefully planned in advance.

There is no reason, of course, why these optional experiences cannot be done by individuals alone, and perhaps shared with one's spouse or a friend. Adapt and modify as necessary, but use these exercises as ways of exploring a bit more fully your own life journey and faith development. When you do, real *faithing* is taking place.

A Group Experience related to Chapter One

Purpose: To help people understand how beliefs and religious values may change over time.

The process described below is a bit complex, so it has been developed step-by-step in detail. We urge you to work through and understand each step before leading the group; you will find it is a meaningful experience.

1. Have the members of the group pair off by twos (dyads) and sit together, preferably face to face on movable chairs. Use male-female dyads as much as possible, but not with spouses. The greatest value will come as spouses, professional colleagues, or friends do *not* pair up, but the effort is made to work with someone not so well known.

2. Give each individual an 8 1/2" x 11" piece of paper, and provide a pen or pencil for those who do not have one. If there are magazines or books to write on, that often helps (hymnals can be used).

3. Ask each person to fold his or her paper in half lengthwise (the folded sheet is now 4 1/4" x 11").

4. Explain that there are many ways of understanding one's faith, one of them being those beliefs and religious values that one sees as important in her or his faith system, and how they may change over time.

5. Uncover a chalkboard or sheet of newsprint on which you have previously written the following phrases, capitalizing as indicated (see #6 below):

Living a MORAL LIFE
Belief in GOD
The GOLDEN RULE
Regular BIBLE study
CHURCH membership and/or participation
A personal relationship with CHRIST
An active PRAYER life
CHRISTIAN responsibility in SOCIETY
HELPING the less fortunate
A concern about...AFTER DEATH

Explain that these are elements of a faith system, with different meanings and significance for each of us. Go over the list, clarifying and providing *some* interpretation of the meaning of each, but do not spend too much time or get into lengthy discussions or definitions. What is important is that each participant should react to these relatively common phrases in terms of their meaning for him or her.

6. Ask each person to rank, on one side of the long sheet of paper, the ten phrases (beliefs/religious values) in terms of the importance of each in her or his faith system. Suggest that they put the one that is *most* important at the top. Then put the one that is *least* important at the bottom; i.e. if you really don't read the Bible much, or have little concern about what happens after death, *say so!* People often feel guilty when everything "religious" does not have a high priority, so help them understand that *something* on the list must be #10. Then ask them to rank the other eight phrases between #1 and #10 on the long sheet in order of priority in their faith system. You may suggest that they use only the capitalized KEY WORDS for simplicity. Remind them that they are ranking in terms of what their faith system priorities really *are*, not necessarily what they "should be" or what they may be for their faith community.

7. Give them about 5 to 7 minutes to do the ranking. When you begin to see that some people are finished, ask the group, "How many are finished?" Normally, about 1/3 will raise their hands. Tell them, "You have about one more minute."

8. After about a minute, say something like: "Those of you who aren't done, go ahead and finish while I say a few more things. When you finish, please turn your sheet of paper over for the next step."

9. Then ask them to reflect upon when they were 23 years old. *Note:* You may wish to suggest that those under 30 might better imagine themselves at age 16, but for the rest, urge them to focus on 23, which most developmental psychologists feel to be the age when most young adults begin to feel an emerging independent image of themselves *as adults.* Help them do some mental imaging with questions like, but not limited to, the following (feel free to use others that come to mind along this line):

When you were age 23:

- What year was it?
- Who was president of the United States (or the prime minister of Canada)?
- Where did you work?
- Were you married? Did you have children? How old were they?

- Can you remember what they looked like?
- What persons, causes, organizations were very important to you when you were 23?
- What images did you have of the future...for yourself? For your country? for the world?
- Other image-building questions.

Spend 2 to 3 minutes leading them in this kind of imaging. The purpose is to help them get in touch with themselves at age 23. Then ask them to use the *other side* of their *folded* long sheet of paper to repeat the same ranking exercise they did before, but this time doing it "...*as you probably would have done it when you were 23.*"

10. Again, give them 5 to 7 minutes, or whatever seems comfortable for the group. When most are finished, suggest three simple steps:

- unfold the sheet of paper so that the two lists are side by side;
- reflect on the two lists: what major changes do you see? Do they agree with other self perceptions you have of changes in your faith system over the years? How do you feel about what you see?
- after they have reflected personally for a minute or so, ask them to share with their partner (see #1) some of the things they see on their sheets, how they feel about them, and what it says to them about their faith journeys.

Give the group about 15 minutes to do this (7 to 8 minutes for each person). Encourage each partner to ask questions for clarification and to help the other as appropriate to verbalize his or her story.

11. When it appears that each set of partners has had time to explore meanings with each other, bring the entire group back together for 5 to 10 minutes of debriefing. You might ask for a show of hands: "How many saw a lot of change?" "...not much change?" (Remind them there are no *right* or *wrong* answers.) Ask if any two partners found something especially interesting talking together such as very *similar* or very *different* scenarios, common themes, generational differences, etc. (One woman in her sixties and a man in his thirties were intrigued by the similarities in their stories despite the differences in their age and their gender.)

12. Close the session with the affirming reminder that change, growth, and development in matters of faith are healthy, and that un-

derstanding the pattern of this development can give fuller meaning to one's present and even future faith systems.

Note: This exercise can be done in triads (three persons) instead of dyads (two persons). It will add the richness of a third perspective, but will also take longer. Consider the option.

A Group Experience related to Chapter Two

Purpose: To help people understand how many factors related to a person's faith development like a tapestry to life.

A tapestry involves the weaving together of many varied threads into an overall pattern with a beauty all its own. Countless elements interrelate to form the larger design of the tapestry.

The Unfolding Tapestry of My Life provides an opportunity for people to view their life development and faith development in terms of both the specific elements that contribute to them and, of more importance, the larger pattern—*the tapestry*—that emerges.

Note: The chart on pages 100-101 can be photo-duplicated directly or retyped and duplicated. These pages should then be given out as indicated in #1 or #2 below.

There are at least two ways to experience the Tapestry in a group setting. Both will be suggested; the group and group leader will have to decide which is best for them. Each model is based on approximately one hour together. For this experience, a longer time is preferable, if at all possible.

1. If it is an *ongoing* group and all participants are willing to do the "homework," the Tapestry and the Instructions that follow can be distributed ahead of time with each member agreeing to fill it out, *before* the group session, at a time convenient for that person.

At the group meeting, divide into small circles of three or four persons, preferably with spouses and close friends in *different* circles and each circle with both men and women, if possible. Each person takes 10 to 15 minutes to share with the others some of the important aspects of his or her Tapestry and how they interrelate as a part of that person's faith development.

2. If it is *not possible* for the Tapestry to be done ahead of time, ask the group to pair off by twos (again, as before, preferably with someone other than spouses or good friends, with opposite genders together whenever possible), and find a place where the two of them can reflect, write, and talk comfortably. Suggest that they each spend 20 to 30 minutes filling out the Tapestry form, then 10 to 15 minutes each sharing with the other person, as in #1 above.

Whichever procedure is used, if it is possible to bring the entire group back together for a few minutes to debrief at the end, this can be valuable. However, it should be weighed against the constraints of time and the fact that some small groups may well want to be together beyond the scheduled time.

Instructions for Use of THE UNFOLDING TAPESTRY OF MY LIFE
This worksheet provides a way to look at the movements of your life that show the things that changed and the things that stayed the same. The following information gives an explanation of the categories across the top of the Tapestry sheet and directions for filling it out.

As you work on the Tapestry, you may wish to make brief notes to yourself, especially if any thoughts or insights come to you. It is not necessary to fill out all the boxes or any in great detail. Simply jot down some key words that will help you recall your thoughts and memories. If you don't know what to note in a particular box, don't worry—just leave it and go on.

1. Starting from the left with the column *Calendar Years Since High School*, list the different logical periods of your life to date by calendar years. For example, those who attended college will probably list "1958-63: College" as the first period in their adult lives. For some, periods will relate to specific jobs or geographic locations; for others, they could relate to identifiable periods of personal or spiritual transition or stability. These periods will often be about 3 to 7 years each, but will vary, and you should be flexible in setting periods. Remember, *you* define them in terms of how *you* see them from the perspective of today.

2. In the second column called *Place: Geographic or Socio-Economic*, reflect your sense of "place" in several different ways. First, what was the physical or geographic area in which you lived (state or province, city, neighborhood) in each period of your life? Second, write down what you sensed was your economic and social situation during each period.

3. The third column, *Key Relationships*, refers to person-relationships you have had that were important to you at various points in your life. Write down the names of people who had an influence on you—on your self-image and self-worth. This could include family members, friends or enemies, lovers, or spouses, clergy, teachers, bosses, etc. These persons may not be living now and, in some cases, you may not have been close to them, or even have known them personally (like a grandfather who died before you were born or a public figure like Martin Luther King, Jr.). Write down whoever comes to mind.

4. The fourth column, *Ways Time Was Spent*, is about how you invested major blocks of your time in the different periods. Going to school, starting a family, working overtime to get ahead in a job, etc. are possibilities here, but it could also reflect periods of time when you did a lot of personal introspection or consciously worked on your spiritual development.

5. The column called *Marker/Milestone Events*, records those events that were significant for you, perhaps major turning points in your life that had a real influence on the years that followed. These could include a geographical move, the death or loss of a loved one, a marriage, promotion, separation or divorce, having a child, a catastrophy but also, perhaps, a moment of grace and joy, a conversion experience, or the like. These are the kinds of events after which things are never quite the same.

6. *Age by Year* simply asks you to record your age(s) during each period. This provides a chronological reference point for you. Fill it out with the same intervals you used in the first ("Calendar Years...") column at the left of your *Tapestry*.

7. In *Events or Conditions in Society*, register what you remember was happening in the larger world beyond your family or small circle of friends that had an impact upon you and your way of seeing and being in the world. Such events as war, depression, the civil rights struggles of the 1960s, John F. or Robert Kennedy's assassinations, the Vietnam conflict, the first walk on the moon, etc. might be examples of such events.

8. The eighth column, *Key Focus for You*, refers to relationships or institutional commitments, or objects of worth or ideas that centered your life during certain periods. Or, put another way, identify what *persons, things, or causes* were of such importance that they tended to dominate your thoughts and actions during various times in your life.

9. The ninth column, *Authorities*, asks the question: "Who or what provided you with authority at a given period in your life?" Another way to put it is "To whom or what did you look for guidance or justification for your decisions, choices, or values during a certain period in your life? (Parents, church, self, someone in #3?)

10. *Images of God* provides the opportunity for you to record briefly, in a word or phrase, what thoughts or images of God—positive or negative—you may have had at this period of your life.

11. *Where I Was in My Faith Journey* asks you to characterize your faith values and attitudes during each period. You may wish to use

terms (Westerhoff's "Styles" or Fowler's "Stages") suggested in Chapter Two, or just note words or phrases that are appropriate ("The naive years," "a time of hard questioning," or "a period of spiritual reflection," etc.).

Don't struggle when you draw a blank...move on to the next box. Relax and enjoy putting together some events in your personal history to form the Tapestry of your life.

The Unfolding Tapestry of My Life is adapted, with permission, from its original form developed at the Center for Faith Development, Candler School of Theology, Emory University, Atlanta, Georgia. The original form of the chart appears in James Fowler's *Faith Development and Pastoral Care* (Philadelphia: Fortress Press, 1987).

THE UNFOLDING TAPESTRY OF MY LIFE

1. Calendar Years Since High School	2. "Place": Geographic or Socio-Economic	3. Key Relationships	4. Ways Time Was Spent	5. Marker/ Milestone Events

Adapted with permission by Kenneth Stokes from Fowler's *Faith Development and Pastoral Care* (Philadelphia: Fortress Press, 1987).

6. Age by Year	7. Events or Conditions in Society	8. Key Focus for You	9. Authorities	10. Images of God	11. Where I Was in My Faith Journey

A Group Experience related to Chapter Three

Purpose: To reflect upon our own faith questions.

Break into triads and get acquainted with your partners. For about 20 minutes, each person works individually writing brief responses to the guiding questions and reflecting upon them. Each member of the triad then takes about 10 minutes to share some of these reflections with his or her partners. Although the listeners may ask a question here or there, it is not really a dialogue. Then, when each has shared, talk together for a few minutes about the similarities and differences in your stories.

If time permits and it is appropriate, reconvene the total group for general sharing about the experience.

Guiding Questions for Reflection

1. Think back to your late teens or early twenties. Did you go through a time of questioning or doubting of elements of the faith in which you had been raised? If you can, focus even more sharply: what was the first faith issue you questioned (six-day Creation, one of Jesus' miracles, etc.)? Make a few notes of what you remember.

2. Did you discuss these questions with anybody else? A close friend? Parent(s)? Teacher? Pastor, priest, or rabbi? What was that person's reaction to your questions? How did you feel about this reaction?

3. Think about the rest of your faith journey since then up to the present. What were (are) some of the other faith questions that have been important to you? Choose two or three. At what age was each important? Do you see any relationship between the questions you were asking and what was going on in your life at that time (i.e. marriage, death of a loved one, going to college, etc.)? How did you resolve that question? Has that resolution been sufficient for you since then? Do you see any overall pattern which relates to your faith questions and your faith journey? If so, can you describe it?

4. Could friends, family, pastor, or others have helped you better deal with your faith questions at some of these times? If so, how? If not, why?

5. How does this reflection help you better understand yourself today and your faith development to this point in your life? How can it help you from now on in your future faithing?

6. Does this reflection suggest ways *you can help others* who are dealing with their own faith questions? If you are a parent of a growing child or have faith discussions with a questioning colleague or have opportunity to counsel others, what have you been doing well? How might you do it better?

A Group Experience related to Chapter Four

Purpose: To explore the similarities and differences between the ways men and women experience their faith and the faithing process.

This exercise can be done in nearly any group that involves both men and women. Adjust the basic directions to fit the particular composition of your group.

1. Divide into circles of 3 to 4 persons, each composed of either *all men or all women*. All the circles should remain in the same room, but separated from the other circles by several feet of "space," if possible. If the members of the various circles do not know each other, take a few minutes to get acquainted (5 minutes). Prepare a brief list of the two or three *main* points in the chapter with which you most strongly agree, disagree, or question.

2. Review and discuss some of the findings and trends in this chapter. Try to arrive at some consensus regarding your circle's reaction to and feelings about them (15 minutes).

3. Reconvene the *entire* group and ask each circle to share one or two viewpoints expressed in consensus. This may be strong agreement or serious questioning, described in #2, or it might be the development of a theme in some new directions from those taken in the chapter. Write these statements on a blackboard or sheet of newsprint—the men's circles' responses in one column, the women's circles' responses in another (10 minutes). If the group is very large, you may have time only for a sampling of responses.

4. Restructure *new* circles *now* with as equal a balance of men and women in each as possible. Again, provide time for briefly getting acquainted, if necessary (3 to 5 minutes).

5. Discuss in the mixed groups several of the responses on the blackboard or newsprint. Try to identify those ways in which women's circles and men's circles respond differently, and why. How do the differences and similarities affect us as individuals, as marriage partners, in family settings, in our faith communities? (15 minutes).

6. If there is time, bring the entire group back together for a short debriefing and discussion of implications (5 minutes).

A Group Experience related to Chapter Five

Purpose: To reflect upon the life cycle as a basis for spiritual development.
Have the total group divide into circles of 3 to 5 persons, and get acquainted as necessary.

Tell them that each circle is going to be an Adult Education Committee of a local church, parish, or synagogue. It could be your own faith community or it might be a hypothetical one. In any case, ask each circle to react to the following scenario:

> This local congregation, parish, or synagogue has an education program involving many adults, similar to the one described on page 57. This program is held on Sunday mornings and normally involves six concurrent study or discussion groups. These are organized in ongoing "tracks" based on the decades of adulthood—the 20s, 30s, 40s, 50s, and 60s plus. Each track has a series of topics chosen as germane to the needs of that particular age group. In each age-group track there is a variety of learning patterns used—lecture, group discussion, field trips, projects, etc., and time frames, i.e. a four-week series followed perhaps by two or three one-Sunday topics. The leadership is provided by outside leaders occasionally, but mostly by the people themselves.
>
> There is one factor that is important: *you do not have to attend the sessions for your own age group!* If a retired couple wants to sit in with the young adults' discussion on chemical dependency, or if the thirties track and the sixties want to have a joint session or two to explore similarities and differences between generations in matters of faith attitudes, more power to them. In other words, *there is flexibility in the structure.*
>
> You and your circle (as the Adult Education Committee) are responsible for suggesting appropriate topics for each of the decade groups. Reflect not only upon some of the personal and social issues for each age, but also on some of the spiritual or faith-related issues that might be significant. What are some of the topics or themes that could be appropriate for each decade age group? How might they be organized (3- or 4-week series, single sessions, etc.)?

Let each circle (Adult Education Committee) work together for about a half hour. Have someone keep track of suggestions. Then reconvene as a total group and have brief reports from each circle on some of its suggestions.

If you have a large group, and particularly if time is short, you may want to assign a different decade, or perhaps 2 or 3 to each circle. After each has worked on it, bring the whole group back together for this sharing.

There are different ways to structure the circles. One is to get people of *similar* ages together in each circle, then reflect on the different kinds of suggestions from the different groups. Another possibility is to consciously structure each circle to have as wide a *variety* of ages represented as possible. Think through ahead of time the best way to structure this experience for your group.

A Group Experience related to Chapter Six

Purpose: To explore and better understand how different individuals may have very different faith development responses to life crises.

This exercise is really a group extension of the first *For Reflection* question at the end of Chapter Six. This question asks a person to:

> Reflect on one or more crisis experiences in your life, either positive or negative, that had an impact on your faith. What happened and how did you respond...at first? Later? What factors (people? reading? a group? personal prayer? other?) were most helpful to you in the process?

For the group experience, the process will develop the theme of this question more fully.

As has been done in previous group experiences, divide the total group into circles of 3 or 4 people, again preferably with spouses in different groups and, to the extent possible, with each circle having a balance of men and women.

1. After each circle has had time to get acquainted, each member of the circle shares a crisis experience that he or she had at some time of life or, if anyone would prefer, the crisis experience of another friend or family member. Remember that a "crisis" experience does not have to be a negative one, but may well be a very positive transition or change in one's life structure (cf. pp 59-60). Each member of the circle may want to make a few notes about each person's crisis experience.

2. In turn, focus again on the experience of each circle member for 5 to 10 minutes each. *Before that person indicates how the crisis affected her or him,* let each other member of the circle indicate how *he or she would probably have dealt with it.* What might have been the faith response of each other circle member?

3. After all have shared what they feel their response would have been, *the original member who shared the response* indicates how it did impact or affect her or his faith.

4. Following a similar procedure, deal with each of the circle members' crisis experiences in turn—first the experience itself, response from others and, finally, how that person grew in faith in the experience. Since it is easy to get into discussions about a particular experi-

ence, have a member of each circle be aware of the time available so that *each member's experience* is dealt with before the end of the session.

5. After all the crisis experiences have been discussed, reflect on:

- how the crisis affects personal faith,
- how different people react in different faith responses to a given crisis experience,
- how a relatively mature faith response may be seen by others as "losing one's faith."

6. If time permits, the entire group may want to reconvene for sharing of their circle experiences and general discussion.

A Group Experience related to Chapter Seven

Purpose: To consider and explore a different way to approach program planning for adults in the church.

"Zero based budgeting" is a relatively familiar concept in business. It means that no item in the coming fiscal year's budget is sacred. No item is continued because "it was there last year." Put another way, every item in the budget must be proven valid and necessary if it is to be included.

We are going to try an experiment in "zero based programming for adult ministry." It is best done in circles of 3 to 4 persons, so structure the group in that way.

The task: Each circle is to discuss the needs of the people of their parish, church, or synagogue and develop an outline of programmatic possibilities, based on those needs, for next year's adult education program. The "zero based part," however, means you *cannot propose anything* that has been done before "just because we've always done it." In other words, the present classes on Sunday morning must be *dissolved* unless your group can agree that there is *no better way* to meet those peoples' needs. If, for example, there is a Mission Study group, it must be rethought: is it, as presently structured, the *best way* to meet the needs of those who participate? Could it be reorganized in a way that could not only provide a more meaningful experience for those people but also possibly reach new participants?

In other words, start from scratch. What are the faithing needs of the people in your parish, congregation, or synagogue? What are some ways, perhaps new and different, that the faith community can use to better help them meet those needs? To do so, what elements of the program can be retained, but perhaps restructured? What needs to go or, perhaps, be radically reorganized? What are some brand new possibilities that might be explored?

Lest this assignment appear to suggest that *everything* must be changed, do not forget that—*for some people in some situations*—it may well be best to retain some tradition and keep continuity with the past. Do not, necessarily, "throw out the baby with the bath water." The purpose of the exercise is to evaluate everything that is being done in adult ministry and to consider if it could be done better and, if so, how?

Have each circle work on this project for 30 minutes and put its rec-ommendations on a sheet of newsprint with a heavy felt-tip marker. Put the sheets up on the wall, with masking tape, and spend the rest of the hour with each circle sharing its ideas with the others.

This may only be a hypothetical exercise for an adult discussion group. Out of it, however, might well come some very good sugges-tions to help your *real* adult education committee in its future plan-ning. Or, maybe, you might try this exercise with that committee it-self. It's worth a try!

A Group Experience related to Chapter Eight

Purpose: To explore more fully the faith tasks suggested and to consider others.

Again, divide the group into circles of 3 or 4 people. There are several ways this might be done for this exercise. Each has merit depending on your purposes. Consider which alternative (or perhaps another) would be best for your group.

- If you have a good age spread, consider structuring the circles to include persons from various age groups for the value of different perspectives; or
- you may want to cluster people of *similar* ages into each circle with the suggestion that they discuss the *faith tasks* appropriate for their period of the life cycle; or
- in a very large group, you might consider assigning one (or perhaps two) *faith tasks* to each circle, asking them to explore it in depth, then share their insights with the larger group; or
- you might let circles be structured around specific *faith tasks* with each individual joining a circle dealing with that faith task that most interests her or him.

Don't feel restricted. These are suggestions only. What is important is to get people discussing some or all of the faith tasks suggested in Chapter 8 in whatever way is most appropriate for them.

However you do it, ask them to talk together about the faith tasks suggested in the chapter in terms of people's lives. How do they see a given faith task being worked through in their own lives? In the lives of others? What other dimensions of a faith task would they add to what has been written? *What other faith tasks would they suggest?*

If you have an hour, let them talk together in their circles for 30 to 40 minutes, but bring the whole group back together for 15 to 20 minutes of sharing before you adjourn, so each circle will be aware of some of the ideas generated in the other circles. You might want to ask each group to write, on newsprint or a chalkboard, *other faith tasks* that they have thought of.

If there is time, or if you wish to schedule an additional session on this topic and chapter, let each circle create its own set of faith tasks for adulthood. Using the "zero based" concept defined in the Group experience related to Chapter Seven, you might want to state that the 14 faith tasks described in Chapter Eight could not be used, at least in their present form. Motivate each circle to start "from scratch" in the creation of their own list of faith tasks for adulthood.

ENDNOTES

CHAPTER 2
1. Westerhoff, p. 96.

CHAPTER 3
1. Weatherhead, p. 15.
2. Weatherhead, p. 21.
3. Westerhoff, p. 96.
4. Fowler, p. 179.
5. Weatherhead, p. 63.

CHAPTER 5
1. *As You Like It*, II, 7.
2. Graubard, Stephen R. in Erikson, 1976, p. *vii*.
3. Gould, p. 78.
4. Sheehy, p. 20.
5. Whitehead and Whitehead, pp. 188-189.

CHAPTER 6
1. Erikson, 1968, p. 96.
2. Aslanian and Brickell, p. 49.
3. *FD/ALC* Report, Part III, p. 35.
4. *FD/ALC*, Part III, p. 39.

CHAPTER 7
1. *IFD/ALC*, Part III, p. 41.
2. *FD/ALC*, Part III, p. 42.
3. *Faith Development and Your Ministry*, p. 54.
4. *IFD/ALC*, Part III, p. 54.
5. *FD/ALC*, Part III, p. 54.
6. *FD/ALC*, Part III, p. 55.
7. *FD/ALC*, Part III, p. 55.
8. *FD/ALC* Report, Part I, p. 54.
9. *FD/ALC*, Part III, p. 49.
10. Gallup & Poling, pp. 79 ff.

CHAPTER 8
1. Havighurst, p. 2.

BIBLIOGRAPHY

Aslanian, Carol, and Henry Brickell. *Americans in Transition: Life Changes as Reasons for Adult Learning*. New York: College Entrance Examination Board, 1980.

Erikson, Erik. *Adulthood*. New York: Norton, 1976.

Erikson, Erik. *Childhood and Society*. New York: Norton, 1950.

Erikson, Erik. *Identity, Youth, and Crisis*. New York: Norton, 1968.

Faith Development and Your Ministry. Princeton, N.J.: Princeton Religion Research Center, 1985.

Faith Development in the Adult Life Cycle: The Report of a Research Project. New Haven: Religious Education Association, 1987.

Fowler, James. *Faith Development and Pastoral Care*. Philadelphia: Fortress Press, 1987.

Fowler, James. *Stages of Faith: The Psychology of Human Development and the Quest for Meaning*. San Francisco: Harper & Row, 1981.

Gallup, George, Jr., and David Poling. *The Search for America's Faith*. Nashville: Abingdon, 1980.

Gould, Roger. "Adult Life Stages: Growth Toward Self-Tolerance," *Psychology Today*, February 1975, p. 78.

"The Growth Dimension: Styles of Adult Learning." Produced by Lindell Sawyers. Program Agency, The United Presbyterian Church, 1974.

Havighurst, Robert. *Developmental Tasks and Education*. Chicago: The University of Chicago Press, 1948.

Lawrence, Jerome, and Robert E. Lee. *Inherit the Wind*. New York: Bantam, 1955.

Levinson, Daniel J., et al. *The Seasons of a Man's Life*. New York: Knopf, 1978.

Massey, Morris. *The People Puzzle*. Reston Publishing Co.

McCullough, Charles. *Heads of Heaven; Feet of Clay*. New York: Pilgrim Press, 1983.

Phillips, J.B. *Your God Is Too Small*. New York: Macmillan, 1954.

Rodgers, Richard, and Oscar Hammerstein, Jr., *The King and I*. Williamson Music, 1951.

Sheehy, Gail. *Passages*. New York: Dutton, 1974.

Weatherhead, Leslie. *The Christian Agnostic*. Nashville: Abingdon, 1965.

Westerhoff, John. *Will Our Children Have Faith*? New York: The Seabury Press, 1976.

Whitehead, Evelyn, and James Whitehead. *Christian Life Patterns: The Psychological Challenges and Religious Invitations of Adult Life*. New York: Doubleday, 1979.

■ OF RELATED INTEREST...

A Purpose for Everything
Religion in a Postmodern Worldview
Charles Birch

Using recent discoveries in the fields of science, religion and philosophy, the author argues for a new postmodern worldview that tackles global problems as well as each individual's need for meaning and purpose.
ISBN: 0-89622-453-8, Paper, 195 pages, $14.95 (order C-34)

Faith, Religion & Theology
A Contemporary Introduction
Brennan R. Hill, Paul Knitter & William Madges

Through the use of real-life student stories and their responses to religious questions, the authors offer an introduction to the Christian and other religious traditions. Special attention is given to issues that arise out of oppression and social injustice.
ISBN: 0-89622-415-5, Paper, 388 pages, $14.95 (order C-18)

Losing God
Michael Paul Gallagher

The author links details of the Magi story with the search for God today to demonstrate how God is found through following the light that leads into mystery. He suggests that God is present in everyday experiences.
ISBN: 0-89622-504-6, Paper, 127 pages, $7.95 (order B-19)

Available at religious bookstores or from
TWENTY-THIRD PUBLICATIONS
P.O. Box 180 • Mystic, CT 06355
1-800-321-0411